MY FIRST
IKEBANA

MY FIRST IKEBANA

Ikebana for the Young and Young at Heart

Louise Worner

Photography: Ben Huybrechts

stichting kunstboek

Foreword

The premise of this book is to guide parents, teachers, grandparents and others in how to teach ikebana to children. My extensive background in education has provided me with the knowledge and experience to create fun and creative ikebana activities for children of all ages. For each topic there is a simple arrangement suitable for younger children, as well as more complex arrangement suitable for older children, as well as adults.

The aim of the book is to foster a sustained interest in ikebana from childhood through to teenagers, and beyond. The arrangements range from simple to complex, requiring different levels of motor skills and degrees of attention. Thus, as each child develops and grows, they can create arrangements aimed specifically at their level of development. Complex and more advanced arrangements have also been included to inspire older children and adults with creative ideas for their own ikebana arrangements.

My intention with this book is to open a gateway for nurturing the next generation of ikebana artists. However, I also hope that, through developing a long-term love and interest in ikebana, children are able to reconnect with the natural world, and become stewards of the environment in which they live.

No book on teaching ikebana would be complete without acknowledging those that have contributed to my own learning journey. I am forever thankful to Yoka Hosono, Master Instructor of the Sogetsu School, who was my first ikebana teacher. I am grateful for Hosono-sensei's undying patience as she took me under her wing all those years ago in Japan. Thanks also goes to Ping Block who enabled me to continue my ikebana journey in Australia. I am deeply grateful to my current teacher, Ilse Beunen who has enabled me to explore this beautiful artform to a depth that I could never have imagined possible.

Only through the unwavering love and support of my family have I been able to juggle writing this book while relocating from Spain to Belgium. My eternal gratitude goes to my husband Shane for his continued love and encouragement throughout my ikebana journey. My passion for teaching ikebana to children comes from my daughters, Amelia and Isabel. As a mother and an ikebana teacher, it is inspiring to observe the growth in their creativity and to see their love of ikebana unfold.

Finally, I would like to thank the publisher Stichting Kunstboek for giving me the opportunity to publish my first book. In particular, I would like to express my deepest thanks to Karel Puype and Katrien Van Moerbeke for all their support during the editing and publication process.

Louise Worner

Table of Contents

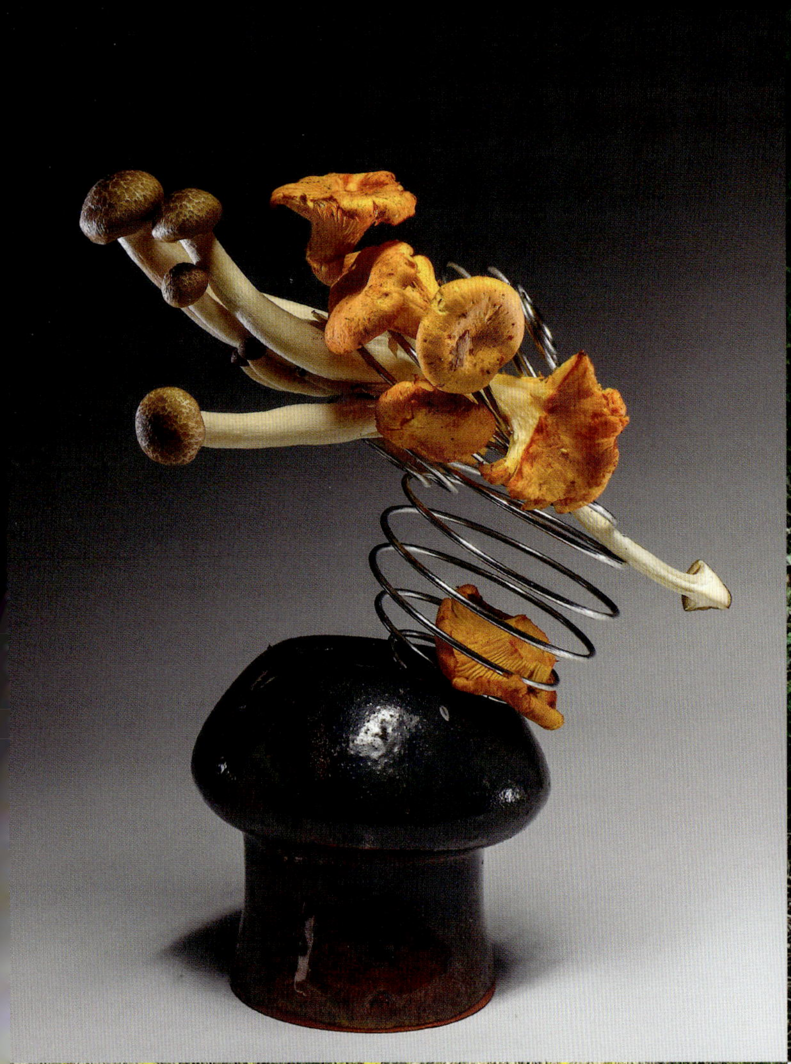
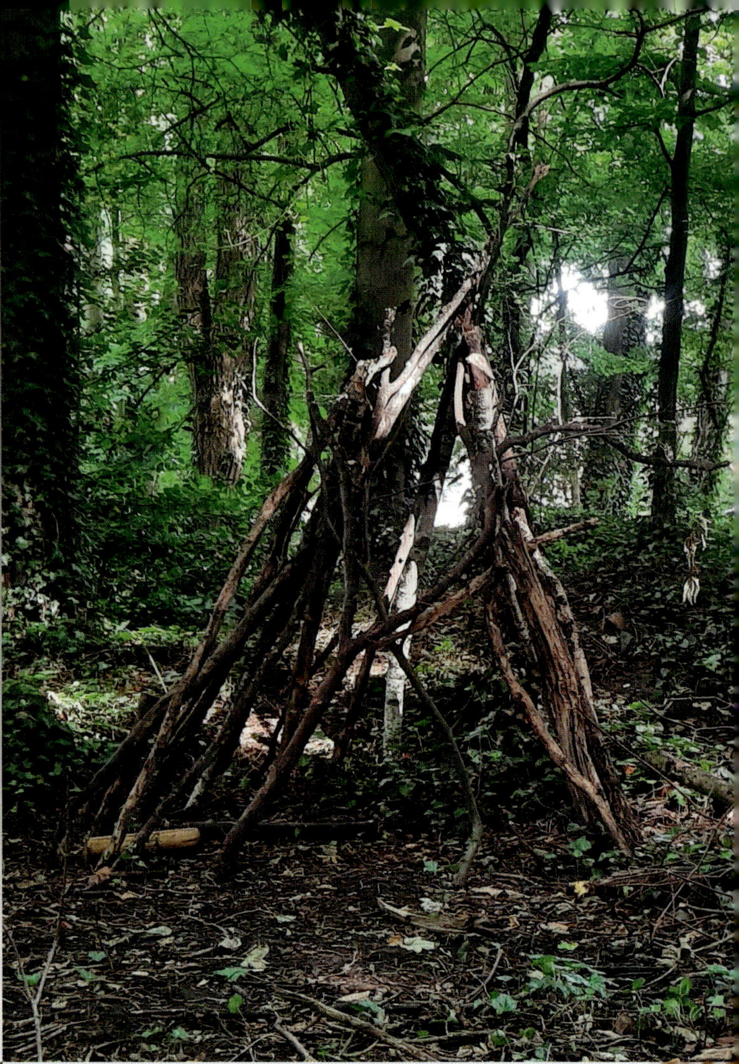
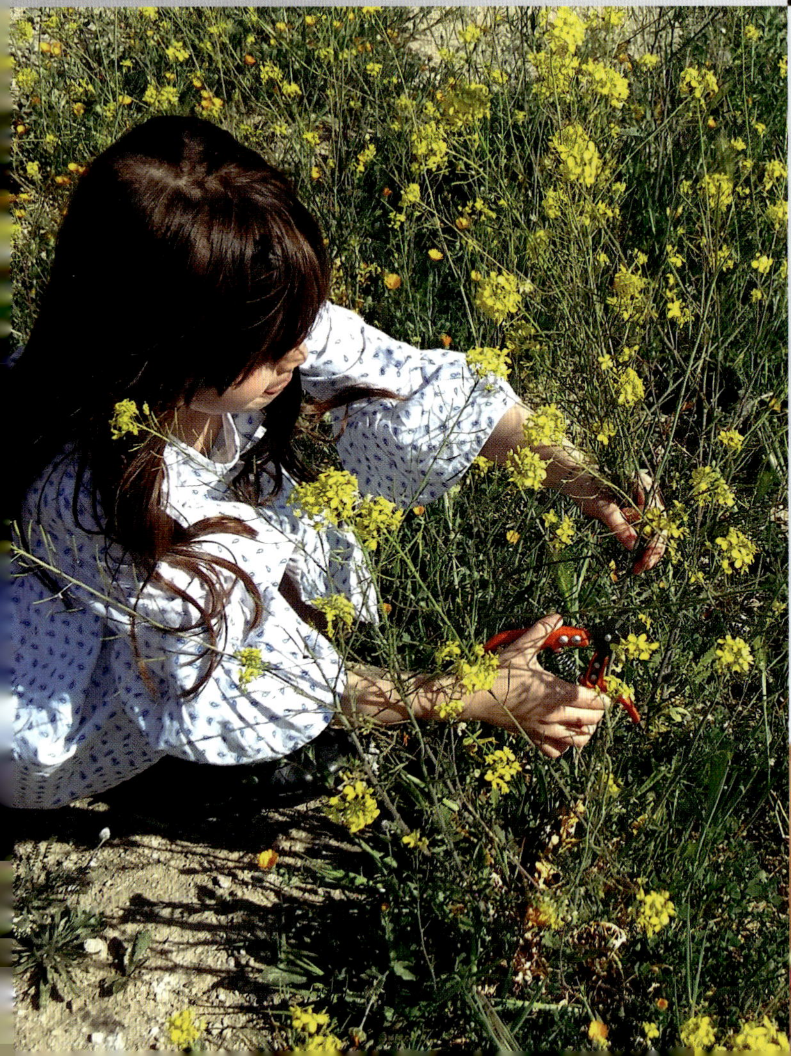
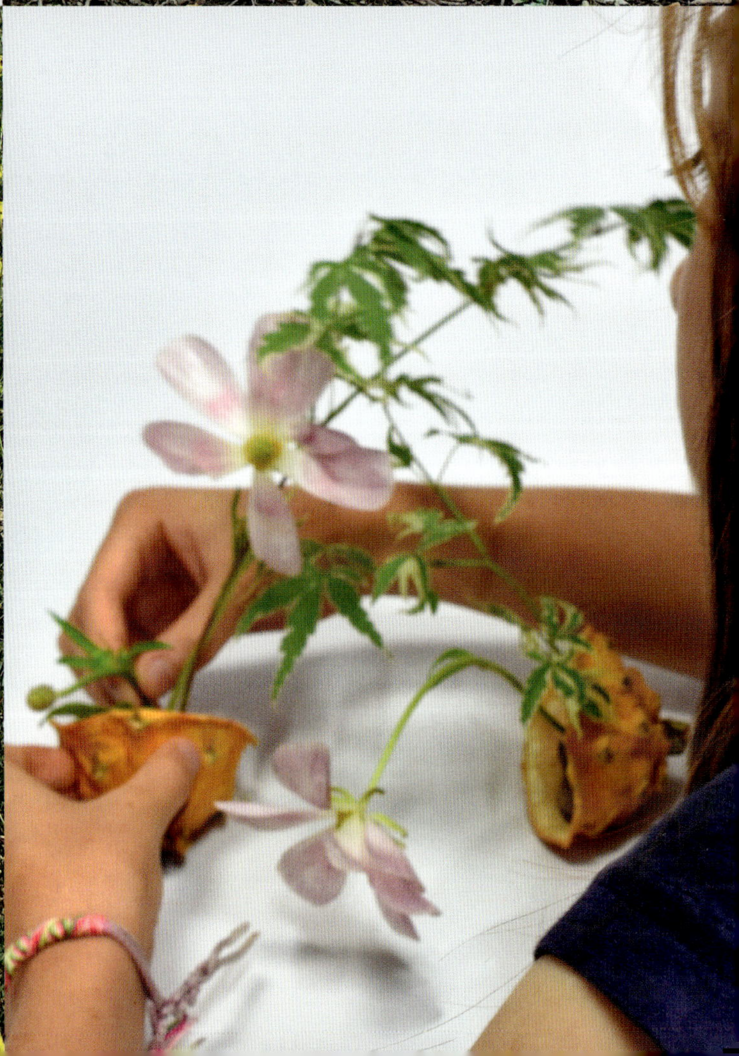

What is Ikebana?

The word Ikebana is derived from two characters, ikeru 生ける
meaning either to arrange, or to give life and hana 花 meaning flower.
However, ikebana is more than just arranging flowers in a vase.
Through the creation of ikebana arrangements, life can be given back
to those plants that have been cut or plucked from the earth.
For many contemporary ikebana schools this philosophy also extends
to man-made materials, as unconventional materials are often incorporated into ikebana arrangements, either in conjunction with plant
materials, or on their own.

No matter what material is used, the process of ikebana begins long
before one sits down to create an arrangement. It begins with selecting
and cutting flowers and branches or, in the case of more modern styles
of ikebana, with the spark of creativity that is ignited when one connects
with unconventional or man-made materials.

History

Despite there being thousands of different schools of Ikebana in Japan, they all acknowledge that its origins lie in the religious ritual of offering flowers to Buddha, brought to Japan by Chinese Buddhist missionaries around the 6th century. These votive temple arrangements, called kuge[1], were placed alongside candles and incense in front of an image or statue of Buddha.
These days, while there are many ikebana schools that still preserve these ancient religious connections, many also place importance on individual originality and creativity. Modern, contemporary ikebana schools base their philosophy and curricula on the creation of ikebana arrangements that are suitable for modern lifestyles and environments. Despite the seeming dichotomy of approaches to ikebana, whether ikebana schools maintain their Buddhist connections, or focus on individual creativity, both approaches maintain and uphold a reverence for nature and the natural world.

Veneration towards plants and flowers is practiced by many ikebana schools in the form of a Flower Appreciation Day. Within the Sogetsu Ikebana school Hana ni Appreciation Day is held annually in March to express gratitude and appreciation for the plants and flowers that the school has used throughout the year.
This respect and homage towards nature is strongly influenced by Shintoism, the indigenous religion of Japan. Fundamental to Shintoism is the belief that the gods (kami) are ever present in nature. Plants and flowers are considered to have holy powers. Evergreens, such as pine and cedar are believed to represent eternity. As a result, they are revered in religious ceremonies and used as yorishiro, a place for the gods to inhabit.

Flowers, such as sakura and lily, are revered for their blooms, while ume (plum) is admired for its adversity, flowering in the depths of winter. Dry branches too, were thought to contain mysterious powers linked to resurrection. In Japan, the notion that the gods are ever present in nature has a profound influence on how the natural world is viewed, and respected.
Despite its religious foundations, the evolution of ikebana to incorporate more secular approaches has enabled it to be more accessible to a wider array of people.

Ikebana in Education

During the Meiji Period (1868 – 1912) many different schools of ikebana thrived and the popularity of ikebana in Japan was at its peak. In particular, there was a boom in young urban women practicing ikebana. In 1899 the Girls' High School Ordinance[2] was passed, thus providing a mandatory middle-school level of education for girls. Prior to the Ordinance, only a primary school level of education was compulsory for girls.

It was deemed that a middle-school level of education for girls included "knowledge in the arts and crafts necessary for middle to upper class life".[3] The government at the time, acknowledged that the promulgation of the Girls' High School Ordinance was to provide an education to all girls with the aim of developing "good wives and wise mothers" (ryōsai kenbo). Women were deemed to be responsible for the home and their family. The government, at the time, deemed that the responsibility for raising the next generation to be of utmost importance for the Japanese nation state[4]. It was within this context that ikebana, one of the three classical arts of refinement, became an optional subject in girls' high school education.

In Japan, ikebana is still taught in many junior-high schools as an optional subject. Although the introduction of ikebana, as a non-compulsory subject in junior-high schools, has its foundation in the Girls' High School Ordinance, modern day ikebana lessons in Japanese schools are not solely for girls.

National high school "flower battles" (hana-ike battle 花いけバトル) are held within and between different prefectures, with the competitions including both male and female competitors. The battles, similar in energy and excitement to Esport GameBattle tournaments, are performed on stage. The profiles and edgy videos of participants and finalists are posted on various social media sites, creating a fun and energetic atmosphere that is enticing to a younger generation.

Why Ikebana for Children?

In our increasingly modernised society, there is a growing disconnect between mankind and the natural world. Most children in the industrialised Western world spend just 1 to 5 percent of their time outdoors.[5] In the United Kingdom, three-quarters of children spend less time outdoors than prison inmates.[6]

In the "Well Gardened Mind", psychologist Sue Stuart-Smith asserts that children who don't connect with nature before the age of 12 are more likely not to connect with nature as adults.[7] In an era where environmental issues prevail, fostering a connection and respect for the natural world in children is an important step in ensuring the stewardship of the natural environment in the future. Kenneth Greenway suggests that the more children know about the natural world, the more they will want to protect it. He posits the argument that environmental conservation is futile without human connection to the natural world.[8]

Thus, in order to sustain a generational stewardship of the natural world we need to create a new narrative which re-addresses our relationship with nature. Our "broken relationship"[9] with the earth stems from the failure to recognise that human society is part of the natural world, thus creating a disconnect between humans and nature.

Ikebana and Nature

"A true understanding of ikebana is firmly based upon a deep awareness of nature".[10] The benefits for children of connecting with nature through ikebana go beyond an understanding and empathy for the natural world.

Deeply rooted in both Shintoism and Buddhism, the study of ikebana fosters a deep respect for plants and flowers. The Shinto belief that the gods inhabit the natural world guides an underlying respect for the environment. Likewise, the Buddhist influence in ikebana is grounded in the triad of Heaven, Earth and Mankind that form a universal whole. Thus, within the realm of ikebana, humankind is not separate from nature but at one with it. Humankind, together with nature and heaven, form the universe.

Even within contemporary schools of ikebana, this duality of Buddhist and Shinto beliefs, underpin not only a deep respect for nature, but also a meaningful engagement with it. By engaging with nature we learn about patience, mindfulness, beauty and impermanence. A deep interaction with the natural world, teaches us about the naturalness and beauty inherent in aging and dying.[11]

Ikebana provides children with a meaningful way to engage with the natural world. It provides a catalyst for change in their interaction and perception of the natural world, training their senses and awareness through active participation with nature. It enables children to focus on the present, providing them with a way in which they are able to see not only their influence on nature, but also how nature in turn influences them.

A report conducted by the Institute of Education at University College London concluded that there was a significant positive impact on the wellbeing of children after spending time in nature.[12] Ikebana provides this connection by facilitating children's engagement with nature. For children, and adults alike, being immersed in nature through ikebana provides the opportunity for mindfulness, to be grounded in the present and disconnect from screen time.

A connection with the natural world is not only beneficial to our health and psychological wellbeing,[13] it can also foster resilience, creativity and independence in children.

Creativity and self-expression

This book aims to provide parents, caregivers and educators with a variety of tools and ideas to enable them to create interactive and meaningful ikebana experiences for children. The ideas in this book provide a resource for the development of creativity and autonomous learning in children. While it might be fun to create ikebana arrangements alongside children, more meaningful learning and interactions with nature occur if parents and educators act as a guide in independent learning. By gently guiding their learning, as opposed to micromanaging it, children are able to discover their own ikebana adventure or path.

Prior to becoming the Headmaster (Iemoto) of the Sogetsu School of Ikebana, Akane Teshigahara had a longstanding career as a kindergarten teacher. Using this experience, she developed the Akane Junior class. Children as young as three years old attend the Akane Junior classes, where parental involvement is minimal.

Drawing on her background in early childhood development, Iemoto Akane suggests that creativity and fun should be the focus of ikebana lessons for children under the age of 11.[14] Children's ikebana classes should be designed to foster individual creativity and originality, while at the same time developing artistic skills and an ability to concentrate and focus.

She suggests that more formal arrangements, as determined by various ikebana curricula, should only be taught once a child is 11 or 12 years old.[15] At this age children have an understanding of angles and ratios, both of which form the foundations for correctly measuring and placing branches.

Process vs Product

In teaching ikebana to children, it is imperative to remember that the process of creating an arrangement is far more important than the outcome. Iemoto Akane stresses that through ikebana children develop self-awareness and self-confidence. She notes that children are able to discover their inner selves through nature. Thus, ikebana plays an important role in the development of children's personalities through the freedom of creative expression. In this respect, she urges ikebana teachers not to over-correct children. Through their arrangements, a child's individuality and self-expression should be encouraged to shine.

Iemoto Akane stresses that it is a challenge teaching ikebana to children. She asserts that this challenge is grounded in the dual responsibility of the teacher, nurturing a child's growth and development in ikebana, as well as teaching the necessary techniques for arranging flowers.[16]

Age Appropriateness

While teaching ikebana to children is a challenge, it is also fun, exciting and very rewarding. It is a joy to watch children grow and develop not only in terms of their physical, emotional and mental development, but also to observe the growth of their creativity. Through their enjoyment of ikebana an understanding and respect for the natural world will flourish.

The ikebana activities in this book have been carefully designed with child learning and development in mind. The activities range in complexity, specific activities are aimed at children in the early years of education with more complex activities aimed at older children or adults. As a result, age appropriateness is at the forefront of each arrangement. The level of manual dexterity and duration of activities varies according to developmental milestones. This is not to deter older children from attempting any of the arrangements aimed at younger children. Rather, it is to give full consideration to the age of the child and their overall abilities, mitigating frustration so that ikebana activities are fun and enjoyable.

My extensive background in education has provided me with the knowledge and experience to create ikebana activities for young children that also incorporate the development of fine and gross motor skills. The careful inclusion of activities such as cutting, threading, picking small weeds, gently placing flowers in small vases, all assist in the development of fine motor skills in young children. Many of the easier arrangements can be implemented at home, to support the development of fine motor skills, or used in an early learning setting as part of a broader early learning curriculum.

In addition, gross motor skills such as bending, walking, running and balancing are supported while children collect materials outdoors, along pathways, in the garden, or walking in the forest. For older children, collecting materials for ikebana provides an opportunity to explore and to engage more closely with the natural world.

My Approach

My approach to teaching ikebana to children is by no means the only approach. However, as with any method of teaching it is an individual approach in tune with my own teaching style and methodology. It is also a style that I have developed over the past 25 years, from my own experiences as a language teacher, from teaching English to refugees settling in Australia, and later to teaching children and adults in Japan. The later part of my career in education was spent as an Education Program Evaluator for the Australian Department of Defence, in Canberra. Understanding and evaluating the "hows" and "whys" of training programs, and critically evaluating them to

develop areas for improvement has provided me with a solid foundation for developing my own individual approach to teaching ikebana, both to adults and children. Prior to relocating to Waterloo, Belgium, I regularly taught ikebana classes to children in my atelier in Madrid, Spain, and in 2021 was awarded a bursary by the Ikebana Iwaya Fund to create a video on Teaching Ikebana to Children.

My own daughters have grown up surrounded by ikebana. A month before she was born, my eldest daughter, "met" Iemoto Akane Teshigahara. At the time, Iemoto Akane made me promise to teach my daughter ikebana, it is a promise I have kept two-fold, as both my daughters enjoy learning ikebana.

Methodology and philosophy underpinning my children's classes

One of my fundamental principles in teaching ikebana to children is to make the lessons age appropriate, fun, and to focus on creativity. For younger children, rather than starting with kakei (the basic arrangements and their variations), I launch straight into freestyle arrangements. Children have no preconceived ideas about what ikebana should be, and, therefore, have no barriers to using unconventional materials. Toilet rolls, empty egg cartons, cut up pool noodles, fruit and vegetables can all be used for ikebana with children... The list is endless.

While I shy away from teaching the formal kakei to my young students, I still focus on the basic principles of asymmetry, negative space and movement, that transcend all ikebana schools. In addition, I also emphasise concepts such as line, colour, and mass that are the foundation elements for modern schools of ikebana.

In my children's ikebana classes, learning the basics of flower maintenance is essential. Flowers are always cut under water, and children are taught to treat their flowers and plant material with respect and care. Autonomy, respect for others, and tidiness is also encouraged, even among the youngest students.

Materials

Choosing the correct materials is essential when teaching ikebana to children. The width and softness of stems are important factors in children's ikebana. Children's hands are small and therefore they do not have a wide handspan to open scissors wide enough to cut thick-stemmed plants and flowers. Flowers such as gerberas, zinnias, cosmos, anemone, and tulips are just some of the many flowers that come in a multitude of colours, and are easy for children to cut with simple scissors.

Being able to cut using simple scissors is one of the basic guiding principles I use to determine at what age to teach children ikebana. My daughters started learning ikebana at 4 years of age, and prior to their first 'lesson', there was lots of practice cutting leftover flower stems in water.

From my experience teaching English to children in Japan, and as any parent will confirm, very young children have very short attention spans. It is important to keep lessons fun, interactive and relatively short. The younger the child, the shorter the 'lesson'. To maintain the interest of young children, ikebana lessons can be combined with other activities such as vase creation, paper folding, painting, listening to music, colouring-in, drawing, or outdoor activities.

Trips to the park, the beach, or walks in the woods can result in creative and experimental arrangements with nature. Arrangements can be made with collections of interesting sticks, leaves, bark, seeds, seaweed, or driftwood. Arrangements can be made in situ as land art arrangements or, if permitted, these precious collections can be brought home and made into ikebana arrangements.

Once at home, arrangements can be made in a variety of cheap and inexpensive containers. Empty eggshells, empty perfume bottles, shells collected from the beach, items collected in the forest (arrangement 10a) vases from thrift stores, empty bottles, recycled yogurt containers, and even tall milkshake tumblers (arrangement 4a) all make cheap and interesting containers for children to use to create ikebana.

Alternatives to Kenzans

I am often asked for ideas on alternatives to using kenzans, the traditional needle point holder used in many ikebana arrangements. Many ikebana teachers have lamented to me that an inhibitor to them teaching ikebana workshops to children is the need for a kenzan, which can be expensive or difficult to source in large quantities. However, as this book will demonstrate, with a little imagination, items from around the home can be repurposed and used as fixations for fun and creative ikebana arrangements. Traditional fixation techniques such as komiwara, tightly bundled straws, have been given a child-friendly twist.

Additionally, I have designed and developed many sustainable alternatives to using single use floral foam. The chapter From the Kitchen introduces the use of paper straws, cinnamon sticks, a kitchen sink strainer, and pasta armatures as alternatives to using kenzans. Repurposed bed springs have been used as fixations in From the Field, while foraged branches are used as a frame in From the Forest. Finally, the chapter on Festivals includes a fun and whimsical arrangement using a colourful slinky to support materials in a glass tealight candle holder.

Our homes are an endless source of items that can be repurposed as fixations for ikebana arrangements. Our love of ikebana can be shared with the next generation, through workshops and classroom situations, free of inhibition.

Critique & Guidance

It is important to allow children the space and freedom to develop autonomy in the classroom. As any parent will attest, even a two-year-old can be fiercely independent. Angst in young children is often the result of conflict between the strong desire for autonomy with the ability to do certain tasks. It often takes children time to progress. For teachers, patience is essential and comparisons with others should be avoided. Each child develops at their own pace. Over time they will develop not only technique, but also a deep sensibility towards their materials. Providing a space for freedom and creativity allows children to think and grow for themselves. As teachers, our role is to guide children in their ikebana journey, rather than to micromanage it. My approach to teaching ikebana to children has always been for children as opposed to with children as they are the protagonists of their ikebana journey. As teachers, we gently guide them along the way, rather than leading them by the hand.

In this respect, it is important not to teach children the same way we would teach adults. It may be intimidating for young children to have an adult hovering over them. When talking one-on-one to children, get down low and speak to them on their level. Although they may fiercely want to be independent, don't treat young children as though they are adults. Children may make mistakes, but it is important to remind them that we all make mistakes, and that we learn the most through our mistakes. Afterall, errors ... are the portals of discovery.[17]

Encouraging children to learn from their mistakes also involves removing the possibility of negative judgment. As ikebana students, we all benefit from feedback, however, when critiquing children's arrangements try to focus on the positives, encouraging them in their endeavors rather than discouraging them. It is important to nurture their ideas, as this will help to develop their individual self-expression. Children may be determined to add more flowers than we deem necessary, however, value their opinions. Take the time to discover what it is they want to achieve and why, and find a compromise for them to achieve this goal.

Follow-up

Follow-up activities go a long way to help reinforce the ideas learned in class. Sketching their arrangements after class helps children to observe the colours and shapes of the materials they have used. It not only assists them to re-examine their work in an objective way, but also helps to develop a deeper connection with the materials used in class, and the broader natural environment.

Now more than ever, children need to reconnect with nature, and ikebana is a wonderful way to do it.

[1] March-Penny, J. (1976) *The Master's Book of Ikebana*, Samson Low, UK p 20.

[2] Ministry of Education, Culture Sports, Science and Technology- Japan https://www.mext.go.jp/b_menu/hakusho/html/others/detail/1317331.htm

[3] Ministry of Education, Culture Sports, Science and Technology- Japan https://www.mext.go.jp/b_menu/hakusho/html/others/detail/1317331.htm

[4] Mehl, M.(2001) *Women educators and the confucian tradition in Meiji Japan (1868–1912)*: Miwada Masako and Atomi Kakei, Women's History Review, 10:4, 579-602, DOI: 10.1080/09612020100200302 p 593. https://doi.org/10.1080/09612020100200302

[5] Jones, L and Greenway, K (2021) *The Nature Seed: How to Raise Adventurous and Nurturing Kids*, Souvenir Press, U.K. p9

[6] Carrington, D. (2016) *Three-quarters of UK children spend less time outdoors than prison inmates – survey*. The Guardian, UK. https://www.theguardian.com/environment/2016/mar/25/three-quarters-of-uk-children-spend-less-time-outdoors-than-prison-inmates-survey

[7] Stuart-Smith, S. (2020) *The Well Gardened Mind - Rediscovering Nature in the Modern World*, William Collins, London.

[8] Jones, L. and Greenway, K. (2021) p 9.

[9] Kimmerer, R. W. (2017). *The Covenant of Reciprocity, in The Wiley Blackwell Companion to Religion and Ecology*, John Wiley & Sons, Ltd. p 369.

[10] Sparnon, N. (1984) *Creative Japanese Flower Arrangement*, Shufunotomo Co. Ltd, Tokyo. p 11.

[11] Stamm, J. (2022) *The Way of Flowers*, https://www.lionsroar.com/the-way-of-flowers/

[12] Sheldrake, R., Amos, R. and Reiss, M.J .(2019) *Nature Nurtures Children, a summary of research for the wildlife trusts*. UCL Institute of Education, London. https://www.wildlifetrusts.org/sites/default/files/2019-11/Nature%20nurtures%20children%20Summary%20Report%20FINAL.pdf

[13] Children and Nature report https://www.wildlifetrusts.org/news/new-report-nature-nurtures-children

[14] Sogetsu Foundation (April 2009) Sogetsu Teachers Association Members Guide, Sogetsu Bunkajigyo Co., Ltd. p10.

[15] Sogetsu Foundation (April 2009) p11.

[16] Sogetsu Foundation (April 2009) p11.

[17] Joyce, J. (2010). *Ulysses*. Wordsworth Editions. UK.

From the Kitchen

Connecting with nature can be done even within the confines of home, as ikebana materials can be found in the most unlikely of places. Cold and rainy, or snow-filled days provide an opportunity to explore the house, challenging children to find items to incorporate in arrangements, or searching for everyday items that can be used as vases.

You don't have to go far to find materials for ikebana. Even within the home, interesting items and makeshift vases can be found or repurposed from everyday kitchen items. Kitchen utensils make for brightly coloured, indestructible, waterproof additions to arrangements, and the recycle bin is a never-ending source of inexpensive materials.

Using household items in ikebana arrangements enables younger children to connect with ikebana through familiar items. A variety of cheap and inexpensive 'vases' can be found around the home. Tealight holders or even ice-cream cones can be repurposed as vases. Empty eggshells, empty perfume bottles, shells collected from the beach, vases from thrift stores, empty bottles, recycled yogurt containers, and even tall milkshake tumblers all make cheap and interesting vases for children to use to create ikebana.

Using items from the kitchen in ikebana arrangements provides an opportunity for children to view everyday items with a different lens, expanding their imaginations as to the use of everyday items, such as using drinking straws as fixations, or pasta as an armature. Incorporating items from the kitchen into ikebana enables children to see the beauty in the things that we would normally throw away, as well as a newfound appreciation of everyday kitchen utensils.

1ⓐ Using kitchen items as a vase: Ice-cream cone table arrangement

It isn't necessary to use expensive or valuable vases when creating ikebana with children. Kitchen utensils and food items provide inspiration for so many different ikebana arrangements as cheap and cheerful vases can be adapted from every-day kitchen items.

While living in Spain, my family and I endured many hot summers. Seeking refuge from the hot Spanish sun, my young daughters played in the shade of our garden. They happily danced under the sprinkler, dodging the droplets of water as they ate rapidly melting ice-creams. While scooping the ice-cream into their cones, an idea came to me. The cones would make inexpensive, fun and portable ikebana vases.

For young children, this arrangement incorporates a variety of fine motor skills from bending the malleable aluminum wire to cutting and placing delicate flowers.

MATERIAL

Ice-cream cone, wire, floral tubes, buttercup, forget-me-not

1 Using flat nosed pliers, bend the wire at a 90-degree angle.

2 Continue to bend the wire at 90-degree angles.

3 Continue bending the wire until the shape is large enough to provide a stable base for your ice-cream cone.

4 Repeat steps 1 to 3 creating a smaller form.

5 Insert a water filled floral tube into the ice-cream cones..

6 Place the ice-cream cone on the wire base.

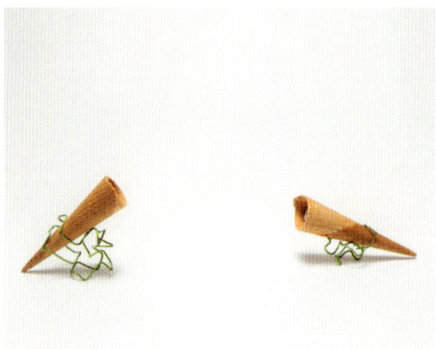

7 Place the second ice-cream cone on the smaller wire base.

8 Cut the stems of the flowers in water.

9 Place a buttercup in the ice-cream cone 'vase'.

10 Add forget-me-nots to the vase.

11 Place a buttercup in the second vase. The flower should be a different size to the first buttercup

12 Finally add a small sprig of forget-me-not to the second vase. The flowers should be placed closer to the rim of the vase.

1b Using kitchen items in an arrangement: Balancing funnels

Within the Sogetsu ikebana curriculum, unconventional materials are often incorporated into ikebana arrangements, either on their own, or alongside plant material.

The kitchen is a wonderful source of 'unconventional' materials. Kitchen gadgets are often made of plastic and are brightly coloured, providing an unbreakable and colourful source of materials for children to use in ikebana arrangements.

The use of kitchen funnels provides a fun fine-motor skill activity for children. The funnels are carefully balanced and inserted into one another creating a quick and fun arrangement for both younger and older children.

MATERIAL

Conifer, Choisya, kitchen funnels

1 Choose a vase, for this arrangement a glass vase works well as it will give the illusion that the funnels are floating in the air.

2 Fill the vase with water.

3 Add the first funnel.

4 Balance the second funnel in the first.

5 Balance the third funnel in the second.

6 Add some conifer to the rim of the first funnel.

7 Add the flowers to the conifer

8 Add a small amount of conifer to the top and bottom of the small funnel. This will give the arrangement balance so that it's not too heavy on one side.

2 ⓐ Komiwara: Using paper straws

Komiwara is a traditional fixation technique. In ancient times, bundles of rice straw were tightly bound together and inserted into the mouth of a vase. Branches and flowers were then inserted into the straw bundle, held in place without the use of a kenzan (needle point holder).

Although komiwara, may provide a sustainable alternative to kenzans, they are rather difficult and cumbersome for children to make and use. While contemplating how I could design a child-friendly komiwara, my mind drifted to the dual meaning of straw in English. In an instance I had the solution, drinking straws. Using paper, rather than plastic, drinking straws, children can easily create a sustainable and reusable modern komiwara.

MATERIAL

Paper drinking straws, Salix matsudana 'Tortuosa', hellebores

1 Cut the straws to fit your chosen vase.

2 Insert the straws in the vase.

3 Continue placing the cut straws in the vase until the mouth is full.

4 Place a stem of salix in one of the straws.

5 Add a second stem.

6 Cut the flower stem in water.

7 Place the flower in the straw komiwara.

2ⓑ Using cinnamon sticks as a komiwara

A more complex approach to the previous komiwara technique is to create a komiwara using cinnamon sticks.
Older children may enjoy using a small saw to cut the cinnamon sticks to size. If a glass vase is used, they can study how water, when it is added to the arrangement, distorts and magnifies the shape of the cinnamon sticks. The use of a glass vase creates a visual effect in which the arrangement is seen inside the vase as well as above it. The komiwara isn't hidden, as it would have been in ancient times, but becomes an important focal point in the arrangement.

MATERIAL

Cinnamon sticks, mock orange, tulip

1 Cut a cinnamon stick so that it is visible above the mouth of the vase.

2 Place cinnamon sticks in the vase until the mouth of the vase is full.

3 Add water to the vase.

4 Cut a stem of mock orange to fit the vase.

5 Insert the stem into one of the cinnamon sticks.

6 If necessary, trim the stem.

7 Negative space has been created by trimming the stem.

8 Cut the stem of the flower in water and insert it in one of the cinnamon sticks.

9 Add a small stem of mock orange in front of the flower.

10 The finished arrangement.

3ⓐ Kitchen sink strainer as a kenzan

When my daughters were very young, they would practice fine motor skills by threading shoelaces through lacing boards (wooden picture boards with pre-drilled holes). The lacing boards enabled my daughters not only to practice hand-eye coordination, they also helped with manual dexterity, concentration, and focus. Of course, they were also very proud each time they had completed threading the outline of their chosen board. The lacing boards from my daughters' early childhood years were the inspiration for using a kitchen drainer as a kenzan. Threading the fine stemmed materials through the drain holes requires the same fine motor skills and concentration as the lacing boards did so many years ago.

MATERIAL

Kitchen sink strainer, mock orange, buttercups, forget-me-not, ligustrum

1 Place the kitchen sink strainer inside your chosen vase.

2 Add water to the vase.

3 Place a stem of mock orange in one of the holes of the kitchen sink strainer.

4 Place a small stem of mock orange at the front of the vase.

5 Add a small stem of ligustrum close to the first branch of mock orange.

6 Cut the stems of the flowers in water.

7 Place the buttercup between the two main branches, and a small stem of ligustrum behind the smaller mock orange branch.

8 Add buttercups to the back of the arrangement for depth.

9 Place a few stems of forget-me-not between the buttercups.

3️⃣ Radiator cleaner as a fixation

I am often asked for ideas on alternatives to using kenzans, the traditional needle point holder used in many ikebana arrangements. While spring cleaning our radiators, the radiator cleaner accidentally became lodged between two of the ribs. As I pulled it out, the twisted structure gave me an idea, the brightly coloured wire and plastic form would make an interesting armature for flowers. Placed in a glass vase, interesting shapes were created by the submerged radiator cleaner. The strong wire structure is sturdy enough to hold flowers and branches, yet flexible enough for young children to bend.

MATERIAL

Radiator cleaner, tulips, maple

1 Bend the radiator cleaner.

2 Bend the radiator cleaner again to create an interesting shape.

3 Place the radiator cleaner in a glass vase.

4 Add water to the vase.

5 Place a stem of maple in the vase, use the radiator cleaner to hold the maple branch in the vase.

6 Add a second stem of maple to the opposite side.

7 Cut the tulip stem in water.

8 Add the tulips to the arrangement, use the radiator cleaner to hold them in place.

9 Add a third flower towards the back of the arrangement, for depth.

10 Trim any unnecessary leaves.

4ⓐ Recycling: Changing the form and shape of a cardboard drink tray

Even from an early age, at school my daughters studied about the importance of recycling. Since they were very young, I have always tried to reinforce what they have learned at school with practical approaches to "reducing, reusing, and recycling". Many modern schools of ikebana incorporate unconventional materials in arrangements, either on their own or combined with fresh plant materials. Using ikebana to reinforce the concepts of 'reusing and recycling' is a practical and fun way to strengthen an understanding of what is learned at school.

MATERIAL

Anemone, liriope, cardboard drink tray, water

1 Choose an appropriate vase. A milkshake cup is a fun and inexpensive option for young children.

2 Fill the 'vase' half-way with water.

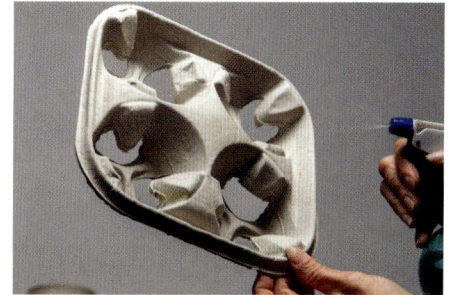

3 Lightly spray the cardboard drink tray with water. Too much water will make the cardboard soggy.

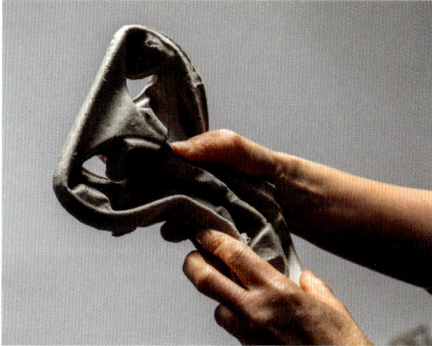

4 Crush the damp cardboard to form an interesting shape.

5 Repeat steps 3 and 4 to create more cardboard shapes.

6 Once dry, place the cardboard in the vase. Make sure the cardboard does not touch the water inside the vase.

7 Add a second cardboard shape to the first, to create height and depth.

8 Cut the stem of the flower in water.

9 Add the flower to the arrangement.

10 Add a stem of liriope to create movement and space.

11 Place a second stem of liriope in the arrangement. Make sure the plane and size of the circle is different to the first.

12 Finally, add a third stem of liriope, making sure the end of the stem is visible on the opposite side of the arrangement.

4 b Recycling:
Deconstructing egg cartons

The use of manmade or unconventional material is quite common in modern schools of ikebana. This idea stems from post-war Japan, particularly in the larger cities that were decimated during the war. Just after the war, Sofu Teshigahara, the founder of the Sogetsu school of ikebana, once lamented that there were no plants or flowers growing in the fields or in the burnt-out shells of houses, just rubble and building materials used for the reconstruction of homes. However, the lack of living materials didn't stop him from creating ikebana, instead he used what he had readily at hand.

Just as we would observe the colour, shape and texture of flowers and other plant material, using unconventional materials in ikebana allows us to see the beauty in everyday items that we would normally throw away. The colour, texture and shape of egg cartons can be just as interesting and beautiful as flowers from the field.

MATERIAL

Choisya, egg cartons, water

1 Cut the egg carton

2 Lightly spray the egg carton with water. Too much water will make the cardboard soggy.

3 Crush the damp egg carton to form an interesting shape.

4 Choose another egg carton in a contrasting colour.

5 Repeat steps 1 to 3 to create more egg carton shapes.

6 Pour water into the vase until 3/4 full.

7 Once dry, place the egg cartons in the vase. Make sure the cartons do not touch the water in the vase.

8 Fix the cartons together using a stapler.

9 Cut the stem of the flower in water.

10 Place the flowers in the vase.

11 Add more flowers to create a mass.

12 Add a single flower, with a longer stem, to the top of the arrangement to create an extended line.

5ⓐ Macaroni structures

When my daughters were very young, they would often come home from kindergarten proudly wearing self-made macaroni necklaces. These necklaces would appear in our home throughout the year, on special occasions such as Mother's Day, or adorned in glitter as ornaments for our Christmas tree. No matter what country we have lived in, threading food items (macaroni, fruit loops, cheerios) on to elastic is a quintessential part of kindergarten education. Many early childhood educators will agree, it is a fun way for young children to practice fine motor skills and hand-eye coordination. Although my daughters have long left kindergarten, they were also reminded of their long forgotten macaroni necklaces when we came across brightly coloured lentil and pea pasta at our local supermarket.

MATERIAL

Bulrush, gerbera, macaroni, elastic thread

1 Thread the macaroni onto elastic.

2 Continue threading the macaroni onto the elastic. You may also alternate colours.

3 Tie the end of the elastic together to form a necklace.

4 Twist the elastic to form triangles.

5 Continue twisting the form.

6 Continue to twist the structure to create an interesting form.

7 Place the structure on the vase.

8 Twist the structure so that it sits securely on the vase.

9 The structure provides a secure armature for floral materials.

10 Add water to the vase.

11 Bend the bulrush.

12 Continue to bend the bulrush to form several triangles.

13 Insert the bulrush into the structure.

14 Cut the stem of the flower in water.

15 Add the gerbera and to finish place a smaller piece of bent bulrush to the opposite side of the arrangement.

5ⓑ Pasta as an armature: Coloured pasta bows

Pasta comes in an array of different colors, shapes and sizes. Children are often told not to play with their food. However, when it comes in such a fun shape and cheerful colours it is impossible to resist the temptation to play a little. The fun pasta bows were used to create an arrangement incorporating line, mass and colour, the underlying principles of many modern ikebana schools.

MATERIAL

Gerbera, coloured pasta bows, hot glue gun

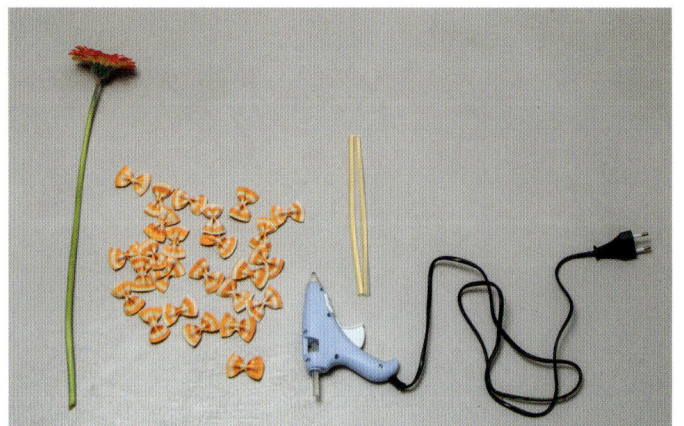

1 Choose an appropriate vase.

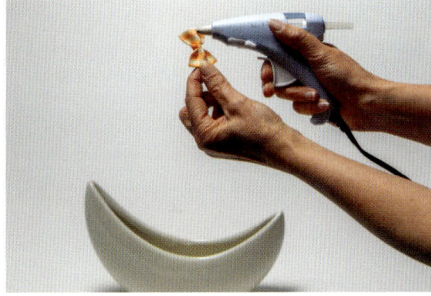

2 Use a hot glue gun to carefully glue the pasta bows together.

3 Continue to glue the bows together to create a structure.

4 Repeat steps 1 and 2 to form a larger structure.

5 Place the structure on the vase.

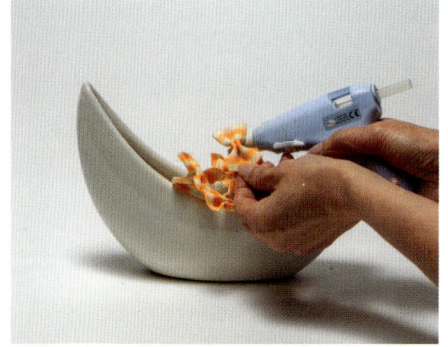

6 Continue to glue bows onto the structure, use the bows to help attach it to the vase.

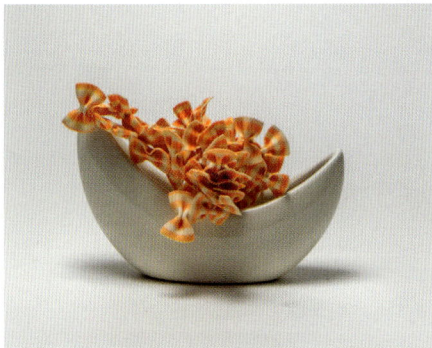

7 Continue to build the structure creating an interesting form.

8 Add water to the vase.

9 Trim the end of the flower stem.

10 Cut the remainder of the flower stem in water.

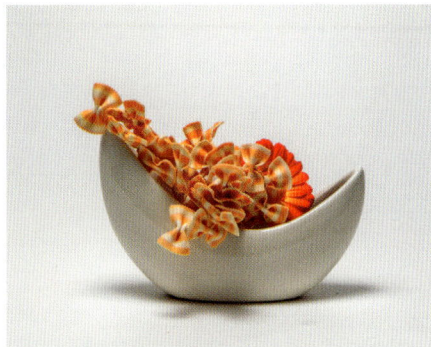

11 Place the flower in the vase.

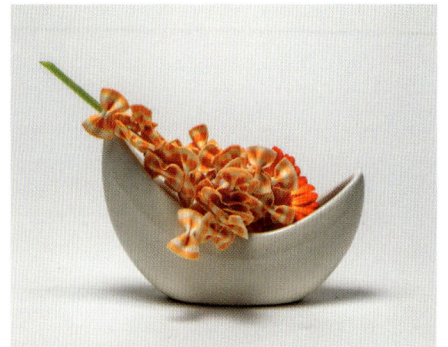

12 Place the trimmed end in the vase, at the top of the arrangement. The stem creates an extension of line.

From the Field

..."When floral materials cannot be obtained ...it does not mean that the pleasure of ikebana cannot be enjoyed"...
YOKOI Toshie, 1986, Ikebana - Fruits and Vegetables, Shufunotomo Co., Ltd. Tokyo Japan, p3

To create ikebana arrangements, it isn't necessary to use store bought flowers. Throughout the year, there is an abundance of seasonal material to be found in nature. Even in the city, small allotments, school vegetable patches, or vacant lots can be a source of materials.

Collecting their own materials enables children to have ownership of the whole process in creating ikebana arrangements. They are able to choose and discover the materials that 'speak to them' and in doing so develop a deeper connection with the natural world.

No matter where we have lived in the world, my family has always been drawn to the countryside. Even in the years spent living in the hustle and bustle of Yokohama, Japan, I was fortunate to have friends that lived in the countryside. While visiting friends in Niigata prefecture, I had the opportunity to not only assist planting rice by hand, but also to harvest the crop at the end of the season. Hands-on experiences with the growth and development of plants lead to a deeper appreciation of seasonality, and the vitality and individuality of plants and flowers.

While my own children have yet to experience the joy of planting and harvesting rice, we often seek out urban farms, or opportunities to pick our own fruit, vegetables, and flowers from local growers. Wildflowers from the fields and hedgerows provide bountiful sources of materials for ikebana.

Often overlooked, even fruit and vegetables can be incorporated into traditional and modern ikebana arrangements. The traditional style of incorporating fruit and vegetables in ikebana is called Morimono, or piling fruits and vegetables. Many contemporary ikebana schools have developed and expanded the idea of Morimono arrangements to also include lessons on incorporating fruit and vegetables in arrangements. Unlike Morimono arrangements, which are placed on a tray, the materials may be placed in a vase and combined with branches and flowers.

Using fruit and vegetables as ikebana materials encourages children to look at fruit and vegetables in a different way. Rather than associating vegetables with taste, they are free to explore sensory elements such as texture, colour and shape and combine these to create fun ikebana arrangements.

For children with access to urban farms, or home gardens, a pre-activity may involve the children carefully harvesting their own fruit and vegetables to use in their arrangements. Or even harvesting vegetables they may have grown at home, or in a school vegetable garden.

Follow up activities might include tasting different fruits and vegetables and describing their taste such as sweet, bitter, sour. Both younger and older children may also enjoy cooking with some of the fruit and vegetables from their arrangements. Transforming their ikebana arrangements into salads, soups, stews or even muffins, and "healthy" cakes such as carrot cake or banana bread.

6ⓐ Using fruit and vegetables: Morimono

The literal translation of Morimono, means to pile up. Morimono style arrangements are created by many of the different ikebana schools or ryu's. Although the rules for creating Morimono arrangements may differ slightly between the ikebana schools, the underlying principle is that fruit and vegetables are incorporated in Morimono arrangements and are arranged on a wooden base (dai), tray, mat, or shallow basket.

For younger children Morimono arrangements may also assist with hand-eye coordination, as they employ fine motor skills whilst balancing or 'piling up' their fruits and vegetables.

Within an educational context, Morimono arrangements may be incorporated into lessons on nutrition and healthy eating, as well as urban farm programs, or even home gardens. An introduction to Morimono may include a lesson incorporating the ideas of MyPlate, a healthy eating and nutrition initiative developed by the U.S. Department of Agriculture, with support from the Former First Lady of the USA Michelle Obama. Reinforcing the idea that fruit and vegetables should constitute half of our plate, children could place their Morimono arrangements on a paper plate instead of a base or dai.

MATERIAL

Padron peppers, radish, onion, red pepper, tray/plate

STEP BY STEP

1 Choose a plate or a mat.

2 Select fruit or vegetables with an interesting shape and colour and place it on the tray.

3 Select another fruit or vegetable with a contrasting colour and balance it on the first.

4 Select another fruit or vegetable and place it on the tray.

5 Continue to select and balance your chosen fruit or vegetables.

6 Finally add your last selected fruit or vegetable.

6 ⓑ Fruit and vegetables in an arrangement

Many contemporary ikebana schools have expanded on traditional Morimono arrangements. These arrangements are often placed in a vase and combined with flowers and other plant materials. Using fruit and vegetables in an arrangement encourages children to interact with materials in a different way. The natural aversion they may have to vegetables such as brussels sprouts, mushrooms or radishes is pushed aside as they are viewed from an artistic perspective in which the importance of shape, colour and texture is considered first, above taste. A second-hand champagne glass was used in this arrangement to emphasize the optical illusion created by water. The transparency of the glass enables children to see the transformation of the shimeji mushrooms as the water is poured into the glass. Transforming the shapes of vegetables through the use of glass and water adds a deeper layer of interaction between children and their chosen materials.

MATERIAL

Orchid, celery, radish, shimeji mushrooms

1 Choose an appropriate glass vase or long-stemmed glass.

2 Place the shimeji mushrooms in the glass.

3 Add water to the glass.

4 Allow children to notice the change in shape and appearance of the shimeji mushrooms.

5 Balance a radish in the vase.

6 Balance a second radish beside the first.

7 Add a few more shimeji mushrooms. They should form a continuous line with the mushrooms inside the vase.

8 Add a small sprig of celery.

9 Cut the stem of the flower in water.

10 Add the flower to the arrangement.

11 Top up the water in the vase.

12 The finished arrangement.

6c Celery as a cross-bar fixation

While kenzans are used to arrange floral material in low shallow vases, they are not used to fix materials in taller vases. In taller (nageire) vases, fixations such as crossbars and vertical sticks are used to hold materials in place. When they were young, my daughters found it difficult to cut the sturdy sticks required for crossbar fixations.

An alternative to help them practice cutting and inserting these fixations came to me while preparing celery sticks for their lunches.

Celery is easy for children to slice and cut, flexible enough to insert in a vase, yet strong enough to hold thin stemmed flowers.

Incorporating celery stick crossbars with vegetables and flowers is a fun approach to including fruit and vegetables in ikebana arrangements.

MATERIAL

Celery, carrots, Hosta, rapeseed blossoms, gerbera

1 Select an appropriate tall (nageire) ikebana vase.

2 Cut a slice of celery

3 Cut one end straight.

4 Slice the celery in half.

5 The slice should be as wide as your little finger (thick enough to hold flowers).

6 Measure the celery against the rim of the vase.

7 Cut on an angle.

8 One end should be straight and the opposite end on an angle.

9 Place the celery cross-bar just below the rim of the vase.

10 Add water.

11 Measure the carrot.

12 Cut the end of the carrot on an angle.

13 Place the carrot in the vase, one end should touch the side of the vase while the carrot balances on the cross-bar.

14 Place a second carrot in the vase (the end should be cut on an angle).

15 One end of the carrot should touch the side of the vase while it balances on the cross-bar.

16 Cut the stem of the flowers in water.

17 Place the flowers in the vase. The end should touch the side of the vase while it balances on the cross-bar.

18 Place a gerbera and another small sprig of rapeseed blossoms in the vase. The end of the flowers should touch the side of the vase while they balance on the cross-bar.

19 Place a leaf towards the back of the arrangement for depth. The end should touch the side of the vase while it balances on the cross-bar.

20 Place a small bunch of celery at the front of the arrangement.

7a Halloween: Pumpkins / gourds in an arrangement

Halloween has always been one of my daughters' favourite festivals. Each year, while living in Spain, we would visit a pumpkin patch on the outskirts of Madrid. My daughters would delight in selecting a pumpkin to carve, as well as choosing several small and interestingly shaped gourds for ikebana arrangements. Over the years, we have developed a tradition of searching for the most unusually shaped gourds. These would take pride of place in our Halloween decorations, and would always receive comments from visiting friends.

MATERIAL

Bulrush, gerbera, gourd

1 Select an appropriate vase.

2 Fill the vase with water.

3 Balance the gourd on the vase.

4 The gourd should be placed so that it feels as though it's floating on the vase.

5 Cut the stem of the flower in water.

6 Place the flower in the vase.

7 Bend the bulrush.

8 Continue to bend the bulrush so that it forms an interesting shape.

9 Place the bulrush in the vase.

10 Add another bent bulrush to the vase.

11 Cut the end from a piece of bulrush.

12 Place the cut bulrush into the center of the gerbera.

7 b Gourds as vases

After the fun of Halloween, we would often dry our leftover gourds to use as inexpensive self-made vases. Once the top of the gourd is removed, children can easily scoop out the seeds. Left to dry, the gourds can be painted in a child's favourite colour and varnished, or sealed with bathroom tile sealer, to make them watertight. Making their own vases is a fun way for children of all ages to engage with a holistic approach to ikebana, as well as a way for teachers to consider alternatives to fragile or store-bought vases when designing ikebana workshops for children.

MATERIAL

Conifer, dried and painted gourd, juglans regia catkins, aucuba japonica berry, wire

1 Place a kenzan in the self made vase.

2 Add water to the vase.

3 Place conifer in the vase.

4 Trim the conifer to create a mass.

5 Add the catkins to create movement through the conifer.

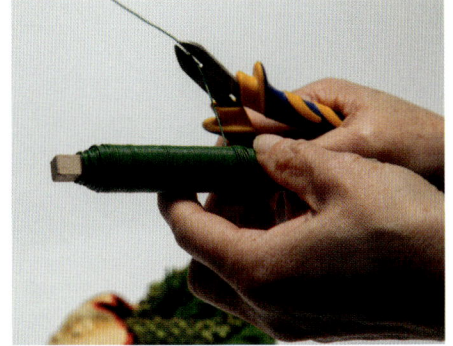

6 Cut a 15 cm (7 inch) length of wire.

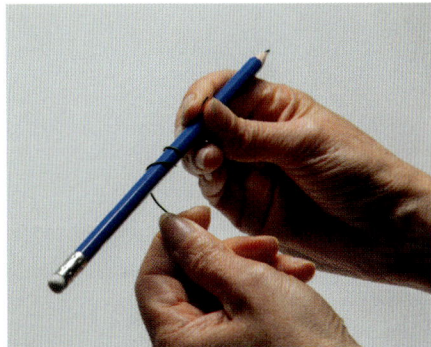

7 Wrap the wire around a pencil to create a coil.

8 Select a single aucuba japonica berry.

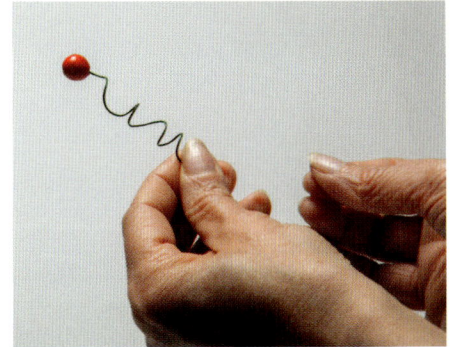

9 Place the berry on the wire coil.

10 Insert the coil into the conifer.

11 Give the conifer a final trim.

8ⓐ Flowers from the field: Mazezashi

Early summer is always a joyful time. The warmer, longer summer days provide opportunities for spending late afternoons exploring fields and slow walks down country lanes. My daughters usually while away these long afternoon walks by busying themselves carefully selecting a variety of wild flowers and weeds growing along the road side. Great care is always taken over these treasures, as they are gingerly carried home to be transformed into a delicate ikebana arrangement.

MATERIAL

Bamboo basket, smoke bush, buttercups, forget-me-not, weeds

9 ⓐ Impermanence: Dry sunflowers

Spending time in nature and watching the seasonal changes in the fields surrounding our home in the Brabant Walloon province of Belgium has enabled my daughters to have a deeper connection with the natural world. Understanding the cycle of the seasons, watching the lush green fields and the forests slowly change colour as the light softens and changes has helped them to understand the impermanence of nature, as well as develop an appreciation of imperfection.

MATERIAL

Spray chrysanthemums, mini gerberas, Japanese maple, dried sunflowers

1 Choose a vase with earthy autumnal colours. For this arrangement, I have selected a small second-hand copper jug.

2 Fill the vase with water.

3 Place a dried sunflower in the vase, taking care not to touch the water.

4 Add a second dried sunflower.

5 Balance a third sunflower on the two already in the vase.

6 Cut the flower stem in water.

7 Add the flowers to the vase.

8 Add more flowers at the back of the arrangement for depth.

9 Add a gerbera at the front of the arrangement, close to the rim of the vase.

10 Add a few small spray chrysanthemums next to the gerbera to create movement in the arrangement.

11 Add two small stems of maple to the arrangement, one either side of the dried sunflowers.

12 Trim the maple so that the stems are asymmetrical (the two stems should not be equal).

9 🅑 Impermanence: Dandelions with a spring fixation

Dandelions are a ubiquitous way for children to experience impermanence. No matter the country, culture or age, no child, big or small, can resist plucking a dandelion and blowing its fragile seeds into the wind.

Of course, my daughters are no exception. Despite my countless efforts to collect the beautiful balls of fluff and keep them intact, without fail, one or both of my daughters falls into temptation and blows the seeds from their fibrous stem. For this arrangement we carefully selected various stages of flower development to showcase the impermanence of nature. Egg cups provided the perfect sized vases, and old bed springs from my daughter's cot mattress were repurposed as an alternative to kenzans (needle point holder).

MATERIAL

Dandelions, bed springs

1 Select two vases. Here egg cups provide a perfect solution for inexpensive vases for children.

2 Insert a bedspring into the vase.

3 Add a bedspring to the second vase.

4 Place water in both vases.

5 Cut the dandelion stem in water.

6 Place the stem between the springs.

7 Place a dandelion in the second vase.

8 Add a dandelion stem for depth.

9 Place a flower towards the front of the arrangement.

10 Add a dandelion leaf extending to the side of the arrangement.

11 Add a small leaf at the front of the arrangement.

12 Add a leaf to the second vase for balance.

13 Place a few dandelion seed balls next to the leaves to create a mass.

14 Add one more seed ball to create movement and depth.

15 I removed one stem to improve the movement and connection between the two vases.

From the Forest

A report conducted by the Institute of Education at University College London concluded that there was a significant positive impact on the wellbeing of children after spending time in nature. For children and adults alike, being immersed in nature is an opportunity to be grounded in the present and disconnect from screen time.

Taking the time to connect with nature is beneficial to our physical health and psychological wellbeing. The Japanese practice of shinrin-yoku (forest bathing) also reflects the idea that spending intentional quality time in nature is beneficial for both physical and mental wellbeing. Studies suggest that the practice of shinrin-yoku reduces blood pressure, decreases anxiety, boosts the immune system, improves feelings of happiness, frees up creativity, and improves concentration and memory.

Researchers in Japan, noted that trees and plants in the forest emitted chemicals called phytoncides, which were found to boost the immune system. In Japan, Hinoki cypress and Japanese cedar release phytoncides, while in Europe oak, beech, birch and hazel were also found to release this chemical[18]. Likewise, research into Mycobacterium vaccae, a bacteria found in the soil, has been found to stimulate serotonin production, which regulates stress and feelings of happiness[19]. While, in South Korea, researchers are studying the effects of geosmin, the chemical released from bacteria in the soil, and the compound responsible for petrichor (the earthy smell after it rains). The research suggests that, particularly in women, the effects of geosmin resulted in a higher state of relaxation and states of calmness[20].

Slow, meaningful walks in the forest are not only beneficial to our health and mental wellbeing, they provide an opportunity to reconnect with the natural world. Ambling slowly through the forest enables us to take the time to use all of our senses to experience what we discover around us.

For children, this multi-sensory experience can involve smell, touch, listening and visual experience. Taking slow deep breaths, children are able to smell the scent of the forest, particularly after rain. They can feel the dampness of the soil, the texture of the trees, the colours of the leaves, and listen to a birdsong.

10 ⓐ Miniature arrangements: Found items as a vase

While living in Madrid, Spain we would often find opportunities to escape the hustle and grind of the city and head to the mountains. The crisp, cool air made it perfect for long slow hikes and foraging for ikebana material. On one occasion, while hiking, we collected a variety of leaves and seed pods. On the ground, we discovered interesting shaped 'seed pods' that we hadn't seen before. Each 'seed pod' had a small hole, as though it was made by a small bird or insect.

After further investigation, we discovered that our 'seed pods' were oak apples, created by Gall Wasps. The small holes in the oak apples indicated that the wasps had matured and left and, fortunately for us, we were left with naturally formed miniature ikebana vases.

These beautiful ikebana vases were carefully packed along with our most precious belongings and made their way to our new home in Belgium. Once in Belgium our foraged vases were inspiration for miniature ikebana arrangements using locally sourced materials from our new home in Waterloo.

MATERIAL

Wild geranium, daisies, weeds, oak apples, tree trunk slices

1 Select two trays for your miniature arrangements.

2 Place the miniature vases on the trays. Make sure they flow across the tray, with a different amount of space between each vase.

3 Fill the vases with water.

4 Cut the geranium stems in water.

5 Place the geraniums in the miniature vases. Make sure there is variety in the height of the material.

6 Create a harmonious balance on each side of the arrangement.

7 Add a small daisy and leaf at the back of the composition.

8 Place a small leaf and part of a daisy in the centre vase.

10 ⓑ Self-made miniature vases

Miniature Ikebana is one of my favourite arrangements to make with children. Very little material is required, and a variety of different objects can be used as vases. I'm often asked for suggestions on the best vases to use for children. Children are the most engaged and have the most fun when they have the opportunity to make their own vases. For this arrangement woody cinnamon stick off-cuts were the inspiration for miniature vases. The aim of Miniature Ikebana is to highlight interesting details within plants and flowers, while focusing on a small part of a flower, leaf or seed. To help children focus on the small details of plants, I usually ask them to pretend to be a 'plant detective'. Using a magnifying glass they need to try and discover the most interesting part of a plant.

MATERIAL

Cinnamon sticks, straws, grass, bleeding heart, buttercup, maple seeds, forget-me-not, magnifying glass, tray

1 Bend an off-cut of straw and place it in the cinnamon stick.

2 The straw should fit snugly into the stick. Repeat the process with 5-7 cinnamon sticks of different sizes.

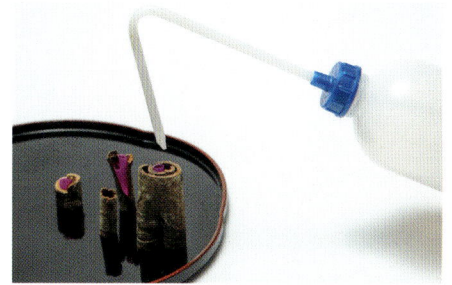

3 Arrange the vases on a tray and carefully put water into each of the vases.

4 Using a magnifying glass look for the most interesting parts of plants and flowers.

5 Choose the parts of the plants that you find the most interesting.

6 Cut the stems of the flowers in water.

7 Arrange the flowers alongside interesting grass or leaves.

8 Place the flowers and grass in one of the small vases.

9 Select other materials that you find interesting and place them in a cinnamon stick.

10 There should be variety in height, colour and texture.

11 To create height in the composition add a taller flower.

12 There should be harmonious movement and flow in the arrangement.

13 Add a flower and grass on the right hand side to extend the movement of the arrangement. arrangement.

14 Place a small buttercup towards the front of the arrangement.

15 Finally add a small flower in the vase next to the buttercup. There should be a feeling of movement throughout the

11 ⓐ Seasonal changes: Springtime ferns

The changes in the seasons are one way of helping children understand the passing of time. Summer fades into autumn, the leaves fall from the trees, the ground becomes frosty and in turn buds appear on the trees and life unfolds again. There are subtle differences even within the seasons. In early spring, narcissus flowers lay low tucked within the shelter of their leaves, by late spring they are tall and lean, poking their brightly coloured heads, swaying in the wind. During our first spring living in Belgium, we enjoyed watching the ferns uncurl from their wintery slumber. As the sun intensifies, the ferns have completely unfurled, the mass of green providing much needed shelter from the sun for many shade loving plants.

MATERIAL

Ferns, anemone

1 Select an appropriate vase.

2 Place a kenzan in the vase.

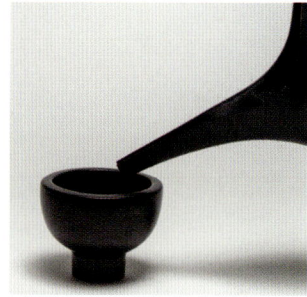

3 Add water to the vase.

4 Place the first fern in the vase.

5 Place a second fern towards the back for depth.

6 Place a third fern towards the front.

7 Add another fern to the side of the arrangement.

8 Cut the stem of the flower in water.

9 Place the flower in the arrangement.

10 Add a slightly bigger fern so that it extends beyond the edge of the vase.

11 Cover the kenzan with small stones.

11 ⓑ Autumn leaves

Autumn / fall is a favourite season in our house. The cool crisp autumn days are perfect for spending time outdoors, on slow walks through the woods. My daughters take great delight in the sound of leaves crunching underfoot. The subtle change in light as the days grow darker create the perfect backdrop for children to appreciate and understand the beauty of imperfection and gain an acceptance of the transience of nature and time. Withered and browning autumn leaves, no longer fresh and green, are viewed through a different lens. The flaws and imperfections of nature are no longer discarded, but become the focus of beauty. This activity can be taken outdoors. With a magnifying glass in hand, children slow down and take the time to notice and appreciate what treasures lay underfoot.

MATERIAL

Foraged branches, physocarpus, leucodendron, foraged dried leaves

1 Select a sturdy vase.

2 Fill the vase with water.

3 Choose a branch and cut the end on an angle.

4 Place the branches in the vase, making sure the cut ends touch the side of the vase.

5 Add some branches with leaves close to the mouth of the vase.

6 Cut the stems of the flowers in water.

7 Add the flowers to the arrangement.

8 Thread some dried leaves onto the branches.

9 Place the leaves so that they appear to be floating in the wind.

10 Place some leaves high and low to create movement in the arrangement.

12a Massing of sycamore seeds

While collecting ikebana materials on a nature walk my daughters carefully placed sycamore seeds in their backpacks. On our return home, they unpacked their bag to discover that the seeds had stuck together. The spontaneous and impromptu creation of mass inspired this arrangement which incorporates mass and line.

MATERIAL

Bulrush, sycamore seeds

1 Select a vase.

2 Push the sycamore seeds together.

3 Place the seeds on the vase. Because the seeds are dry they do not require water.

4 Add more seeds to create a mass.

5 Place a stem of bulrush through the seeds. There should be a strong upwards movement.

6 Place a sycamore seed in front of the bulrush to hide the point where it was placed on the sycamore seeds.

12ⓑ Intersecting pine cones

We often collect a variety of ikebana materials while on hikes in the forest and mountains. For young children, exploring nature on uneven paths, clambering over fallen trees, bending down to collect materials, and navigating tree roots and rocks all contribute towards the development of gross motor skills.

The development of gross motor skills, movements that involve the large muscles in the torso, arms and legs, are important for core stability. Activities promoting gross motor skill development are not only essential to performing everyday tasks, but also form the foundation for the development of fine motor skills through reaction speed, balance and strength.

Beguilingly simplistic, this arrangement enables children to practice both gross and fine motor skills. Collecting the materials outdoors provides opportunities for children to practice gross motor skills, while carefully placing and intersecting colored sticks in the ridges of the pinecones assists with the practice of fine motor skills.

MATERIAL

Gerbera, pine cones, coloured sticks

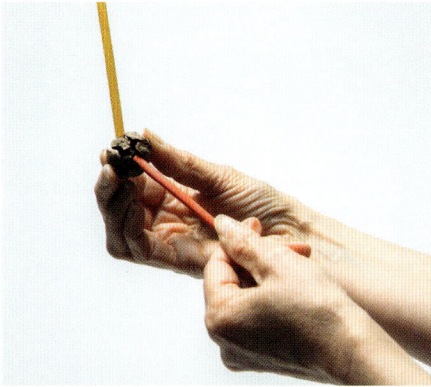

1 Insert the sticks into the pine cones.

2 Make sure that the sticks are secure.

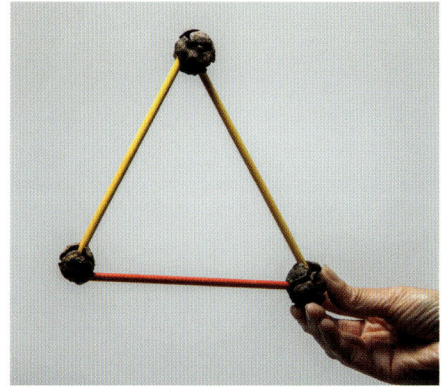

3 Join the sticks and pinecones together to form different shapes.

4 Use one of the sticks without a pinecone to place the structure in your chosen vase.

5 Cut the stem of the gerbera in water.

6 Place the flower in the vase.

13a Foraged branches: Branches as a fixation

I am always thinking about alternatives to using kenzans that are appropriate for both children and adults. While on holiday in Portugal, I spotted rows of agave with tall and dried inflorescences. Some had fallen to the ground, and I couldn't resist collecting a few. As I bundled them into the back of the car, an idea came to me. They would make an interesting armature particularly in combination with one of the Portuguese ceramic bowls bought the day before.

MATERIAL

Dried agave inflorescences, anthurium, ligustrum

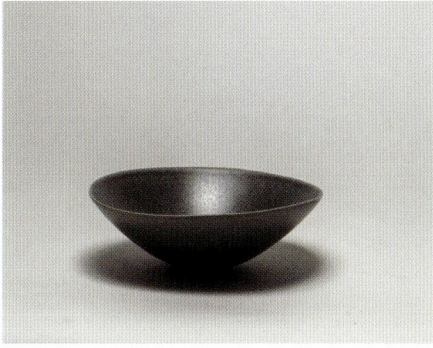

1 Select a low wide vase or bowl.

2 Place a branch across the vase so that it extends from one side to the other.

3 Intertwine a few small branches to create depth.

4 Add a few more small branches to create height.

5 Add water to the bowl.

6 Using the dried branches as an armature, add a few branches of ligustrum. Ensure that they extend beyond the rim of the vase.

7 Add more ligustrum at the back of the arrangement, to create depth.

8 Cut the stem of the flower in water.

9 Place the flower in the vase, using the dried branches as support. Add a small branch of ligustrum at the front.

13b Foraged branches: Bare branches

We don't often associate winter with inspiring ikebana, however, bare branches in winter are an inspiration for studying negative space, or *ma* (間). Prior to creating their arrangements, children may wish to sit or lie on a park bench and sketch the empty spaces between the branches of the trees.

Negative space is an integral part of every ikebana arrangement, it is as important and intentional as the branches and flowers in the arrangement. However, intangible concepts such as 'nothingness' or emptiness are difficult for children to comprehend. When emptiness is framed, it becomes tangible and can thus be visualized by children. Drawing the space between the trees reinforces the concept of emptiness in a concrete way.

MATERIAL

Foraged branch, typha leaf, allium

1 Select a tall vase with a narrow opening.

2 Carefully study the bare branch to discover the most beautiful angle.

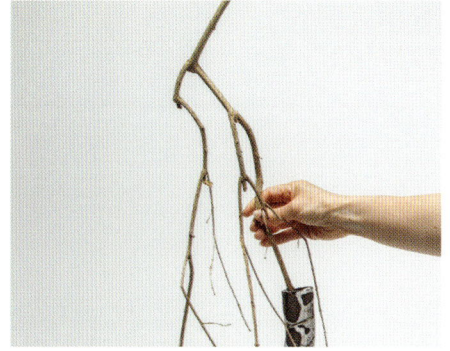

3 The most beautiful angle may not be the way the branch grows in nature.

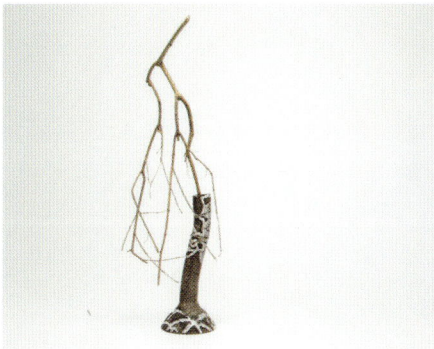

4 Place the branch in the vase.

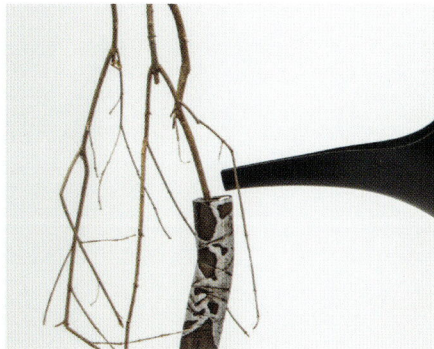

5 Add water to the vase.

6 Cut the stem of the flower in water.

7 Place the allium in the vase

8 Add the typha leaf, curving it from the back to the front of the arrangement.

14ⓐ Parts of a tree: Leaves

The activity can be incorporated into the study of trees and plants, or a unit on the seasons. It may also be incorporated into summer camp activities, helping students to identify trees and have a greater understanding of, and a relationship with, the local environment.

For children of all ages, leaf identification cards (a picture of a leaf with the name on it) can be used to help them identify a specific leaf. Each child could be given a different leaf, or at home a different leaf could be used each time the child goes on a nature walk. Within this context, children may wish to examine and discuss the various shapes of leaves; oval, heart shaped, oblong, triangular, elliptical, their colours or any distinctive characteristics that they have noticed.

Older children may wish to create their own leaf identification catalogue - collecting deciduous leaves, researching and identifying each leaf after collection. Within the context of a science class, a dichotomous tree key may be used to help with identifying the types of trees, identifying simple or compound leaves, lobed/unlobed leaves,

For workshops, a leaf identification card could include 6-9 different leaves (with names). The cards could be used as part of a treasure hunt in which children have to explore and look for each leaf. Colouring them in as they find them.

The types of leaves will vary depending on your local area and climate. Northern hemisphere examples might include: Ginkgo, Maple, Beech, Ash, Oak, Chestnut.

MATERIAL

Acer rubrum, spray chrysanthemum, hole punch

1 Select a glass vase.

2 Add water to the vase.

3 Use a hole punch to create holes in the leaf.

4 Create several holes in the leaf.

5 The leaf should have areas of positive and negative space - areas with holes and without holes.

6 Carefully fold the leaf and place it in the vase.

7 Ensure the stem remains outside the vase.

8 Gently fold the stem, securing it through the leaf.

9 Inside the vase, there should be an area of negative space (emptiness without any leaf).

10 Dip your finger in water to stick the leaf holes on the vase.

11 Stick the leaf holes on the surface of the vase, in the area of negative space.

12 Cut the stem of the flower in water.

13 Add a flower and grass on the right hand side to extend the movement of the arrangement.

14 Place a small buttercup towards the front of the arrangement.

15 Finally add a small flower in the vase next to the buttercup. There should be a feeling of movement throughout the arrangement.

14ⓑ Parts of a tree: Bark

We often identify different types of trees through their leaves. However, an alternative way to identify trees is by looking at their bark. Examining the color and texture of tree bark enables children to slow down and engage with nature in a tactile and textural way.

A fun and alternative way to engage with the different characteristics of bark, as well as experimenting with a different art technique, is to do tree bark rubbings.

Bark rubbings reveal the different textures and patterns of trees. On close inspection, children are able to discover that the bark of cherry trees is shiny with deep red grooves, while beech trees are light grey and smooth. Sycamore bark resembles camouflage, while some species of eucalyptus have bark that is long and stringy.

Taking the time to look closely at trees, and noticing these different characteristics, provides children with alternative markers for tree identification, and enables them to connect with the natural world in a different way. Follow-up activities, or ways to reinforce the knowledge gained might include a tree bark treasure hunt, or tree bark bingo. Older children may enjoy making their own bingo cards or treasure hunt cards using their tree bark rubbings.

MATERIAL

Eucalyptus bark, mock orange, freesias

1 Choose a vase and add water.

2 Place a piece of eucalyptus bark in the vase. Take care that the bark does not touch the water.

3 Cut the stem of the flower in water.

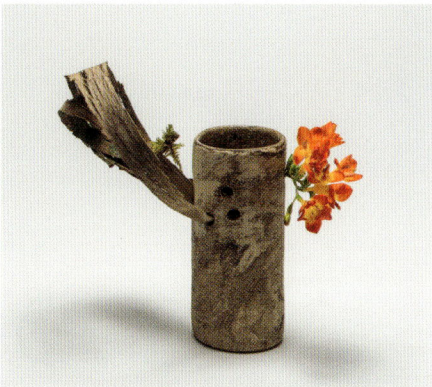

4 Place the flower in the vase.

5 Add more flowers to create a mass.

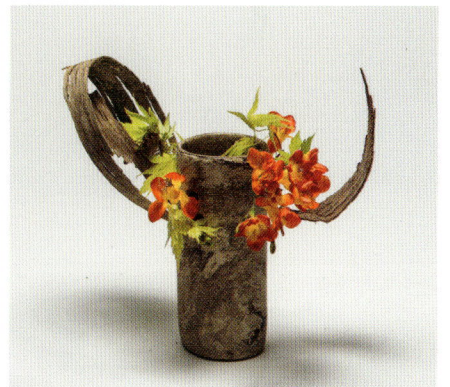

6 Add a second piece of eucalyptus bark on the opposite side. Add a few flowers to the front and some small branches of mock orange for movement.

14c Parts of a tree: Tree trunk

We often mark our children's growth and development on a growth chart and each year growth is compared. Some years it seems as though the increments are small, whilst, in others, growth seems to be rapid and sudden. Just like children, the story of a tree's growth can be seen through the growth rings on the wood. Walking through the forest we often come across felled trees, taking the time to look carefully at the tree trunk and count the rings enables children to have a deeper connection with the natural world. Understanding the age of trees in comparison to their own age provides children with a different perspective of the natural world, and their place within it.

MATERIAL

Tree trunk slices, aucuba japonica, typha leaf, slices of cork, glue gun

1 Select a vase, preferably with a split opening.

2 Cut the cork into slices.

3 A hot glue gun is a fast and efficient way to glue the slices of tree.

4 Glue a slice of cork onto a slice of tree trunk.

5 Glue a second tree trunk to the back of the cork.

6 Continue to glue slices of cork and trunk together to form a structure.

7 Place the structure in the vase.

8 Add water to the vase, making sure the water does not reach the slices of wood and cork.

9 Add a small stem of aucuba japonica to the arrangement. Try not to conceal the wooden structure.

10 Add a few leaves of aucuba japonica to the opposite side, remember that there is harmony in imbalance.

11 Cut a typha leaf in two unequal parts.

12 Add the tip of the typha leaf to the side of the arrangement with fewer leaves. and the end of the typha leaf to the opposite side. The line created should appear to be continuous.

For Festivals

The influence of Shintoism in Japan is profound, with specific plants and flowers playing a significant and symbolic role in many festivals. Even in modern day Japan, the symbolic and spiritual meaning associated with certain plants dictates not only how and when they are used in festival decorations, but also how and when they are disposed of.

In Japan, January is often referred to as the month of pine. In the lead up to, and during the New Year period, pine is often used in New Year's ikebana arrangements, and decorations. In Shintoism, evergreens such as pine, cedar or cypress are considered sacred as the gods (Toshigami-sama 年神様) would inhabit them during the New Year period, bringing luck. Pairs of decorations called Kadomatsu 門松, flank doorways and entrances, providing the gods a welcome place to reside (yorishiro) during the first month of the year.

Traditionally pine, bamboo and plum are used in Kadomatsu. Considered to be auspicious, they each hold symbolic meaning. Evergreens such as pine represent eternity, bamboo symbolises good luck, longevity, strength and flexibility, while plum blossoms appear, against all adversity, in the depths of winter. These three plants are often referred to as the "Three Friends of Winter".

As it is believed that the gods reside in the Kadomatsu during the New Year period, there is a specific ritual for their disposal. When I lived in Yokohama, Kadomatsu were removed from the entrance ways of homes and businesses after the 7th January. New Year's decorations were taken to our local temple where we were able to burn them in a specially designated area. This ritual burning of all New Year's decorations meant that the gods could be released from their earthly abode.

In Japan, New Years Day is one of the five seasonal festivals (五節句, gosekku) held on auspicious dates throughout the year (1st January, 3rd March, 5th May, 7th July, 9th September). Hina-matsuri (雛祭り), Girls' Day/ Dolls' Day is celebrated on March 3rd, Children's Day (Kodomo no hi), previously known as Boy's Day (Tango-no-Sekku), is celebrated in Japan on 5th of May, Tanabata (七夕), the Star Festival on the 7th of July, and Chrysanthemum Day on the 9th of September. Since 2021, the 6th of June has been designated as Ikebana Day. The date was chosen by the Japan Ikebana Art Association to promote the spread of ikebana. It is also a day which is considered auspicious for 6 year olds to commence artistic endeavors, particularly the traditional arts.

Creating ikebana arrangements for these different seasonal festivals is a fun way for children to gain a deeper understanding of Japanese culture. However, it is also interesting for children to understand how ikebana can relate to their own culture, as well as the customs and festivals of others. Arrangements celebrating spring might include festivals such as Carnivale or Holi (the Festival of Colours). Christmas ikebana arrangements may add an extra festive touch to the decorations that adorn many homes during December.

15ⓐ Japanese New Year's arrangements: Bamboo and mandarin

New Year's was one of my favourite festivals while living in Japan. I always enjoyed the coming together of friends and family on New Year's Eve. Prior to heading out in the bitter cold we would make Toshikoshi soba. Across Japan, on the 31st December families would eat Toshikoshi soba as the long noodles represent a long life as well as symbolising good fortune for the year ahead. Always memorable was the midnight visit to Sojiji temple, one of the main temples of Soto Zen Buddhism and a stone's throw from where I used to live. We would wait patiently in the cold for our turn to draw back the huge log to sound the bell. During the evening, the bell would toll 108 times as part of the Buddhist ritual Joya no Kane. This annual symbolic ritual represents the cleansing of the 108 worldly desires that a person may experience in their lifetime. After the bell is struck for the final time, it is believed that you will be cleansed of your worries from the previous year. As soon as the clock struck twelve, we would walk across to our local Shinto Shrine to welcome the new year and make wishes for the year ahead.

New Year's ikebana arrangements are also highly symbolic with each material having an important meaning. Bamboo (take) symbolises good luck, longevity, strength and flexibility. Evergreens such as pine, cedar or cypress are considered sacred in Shintoism as the gods would inhabit them during the New Year period. Mikans (tangerines) are also symbolic representing wealth and during the New Year are often displayed atop two mochi rice cakes.

MATERIAL

Bamboo, conifer/pine, mandarins, vinegar, cotton wool

1 Select an appropriate vase.

2 Cut the bamboo and dip the end in vinegar for 10 mins. This will help to preserve the leaves.

3 Add water to the vase.

4 Place the bamboo in the vase.

5 To help stabilize the bamboo, push a little cotton wool between the bamboo and the vase.

6 Place cotton wool all the way around the bamboo for extra stability.

7 The bamboo should be stable and stand straight in the vase.

8 Place pine or conifer close to the mouth of the vase.

9 Add a small branch of pine/conifer to the back of the arrangement for depth.

10 Balance a mandarin next to the bamboo.

11 Balance a second mandarin on top of the first.

15 ⓑ Complex New Year's arrangement: Making mizuhiki

Mizuhiki, long twisted lengths of rice paper, are often used in New Year ikebana arrangements. Red and white, or gold and silver threads are used for celebrations and can often be seen in New Year's ikebana arrangements. It can be difficult to buy mizuhiki outside of Japan. While creating ikebana arrangements for the New Year I decided to try my hand at creating my own. Shredded New Zealand flax (phormium) has often been used in ikebana arrangements. With this in mind, I decided to paint the dried flax gold to create a homemade version of mizuhiki.

MATERIAL

Phormium, conifer/pine, orchid, kenzan, cutting board, paint, paintbrush, New Year's decoration

1 Select an appropriate vase. Here I have chosen a bamboo vase due to the symbolic relevance of bamboo in New Year's arrangements.

2 Place a phormium leaf on a cutting mat.

3 Use a kenzan to shred the phormium leaf.

4 Continue shredding the leaf until fine lines are formed.

5 Make sure the lines are equal in width.

6 Once dry, paint the shredded leaf with water based poster paints and allow to dry.

7 Fill the vase with water.

8 Bend the painted leaf.

9 Place the curved, shredded phormium leaf in the vase.

10 Secure the end of the leaf in the vase.

11 Place a second phormium 'mizuhiki' in the vase.

12 Add a small branch of pine/conifer to the arrangement.

13 Add more pine/conifer for depth.

14 Add a smaller branch of pine/conifer to the opposite side.

15 Cut the stem of the flower in water.

16 Place the flower in the vase.

17 Trim the phormium mizuhiki so that there aren't any stray ends.

18 The mizuhiki should look neat and smooth.

16 ⓐ Celebrating spring Carnival: Using a slinky to hold material

Carnival takes place in late February or early March, usually in the week prior to Lent. It is celebrated with a week of indulgence, celebration and fun before the restrictions of Lent.

When we lived in Spain, my children would celebrate Carnival at school by wearing fancy dress costumes. While in Madrid city centre, festivities took the form of parades, musical events, a Masquerade Ball, and street performances. Carnival has always been a festival filled with fun, colour and whimsy.

For this arrangement, I wanted to explore using a colourful slinky as an alternative to a kenzan. Younger children can easily manipulate the slinky, and once placed in a clear vase, they can explore the way that water distorts the materials submerged inside it, just as funfair mirrors distort their reflections.

MATERIAL

Narcissus leaves, tulips, colourful plastic slinky

1 Choose a clear glass vase. Here I have used a tea light holder, which is an inexpensive option for children.

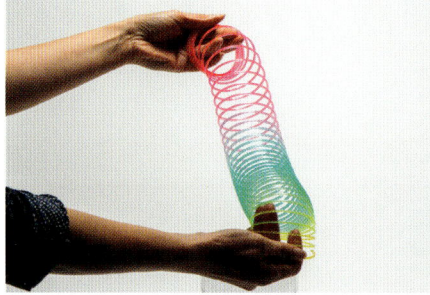

2 Unravel the slinky.

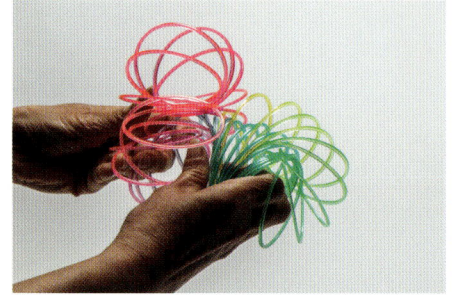

3 Twist the slinky to create different forms and shapes.

4 Place the slinky in the vase, making sure that part is submerged inside the vase and part is out of the vase.

5 Add water to the vase. Children may enjoy watching the slinky change shape as the water is added to the vase.

6 Cut the stem of the tulip in water.

7 Place the tulip in the vase, using the slinky as an armature.

8 Split the narcissus leaves lengthways.

9 Add the narcissus leaves, using the slinky to secure it in the arrangement.

10 Repeat steps 8 and 9, creating movement with the narcissus leaves.

11 Continue to add split narcissus leaves. Make sure there is variety in the size of the circles and angles they are placed at.

12 Finally add a longer narcissus leaf close to the tulip.

16 ⓑ Holi: Coloured straws

The advent of spring is celebrated in different ways throughout the world. Across India, the festival of Holi is a colourful and joy-filled celebration of the arrival of spring, and the end of winter. Known as the festival of colours, it is a Hindu festival celebrating eternal love as well as the triumph of good over evil. Holi is a playful festival, in celebration of the many colors of spring, coloured water, or powder is thrown at friends or strangers in jest.

Although Holi is predominantly celebrated in India, through the Indian diaspora it is celebrated in many countries throughout the world. My daughters have had the joy of experiencing the explosion of colours associated with the Festival of Holi in both Australia and Spain. The riotous fun experienced by my children when spraying friends with coloured powder was the inspiration for this fun filled, explosive, and joyful arrangement.

MATERIAL

Gerberas, coloured straws, pencil erasers, loom bands, crochet hook

1 Select three bright and colourful vases.

2 Add water to the vases. It will help with stability

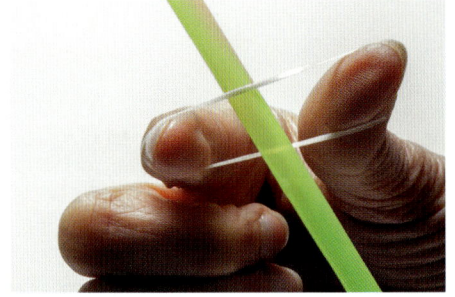

3 Place a loom band over the straw.

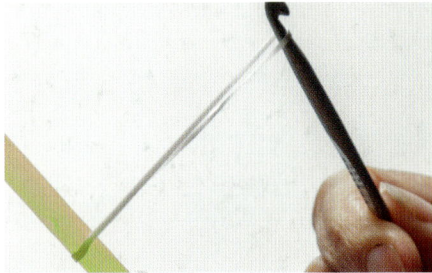

4 Use a crochet hook to pull the band.

5 Place a second straw across the first and secure it to the first with the band.

6 Hook the band over the end of the first straw to secure the straws together.

7 The straws should be fastened together securely.

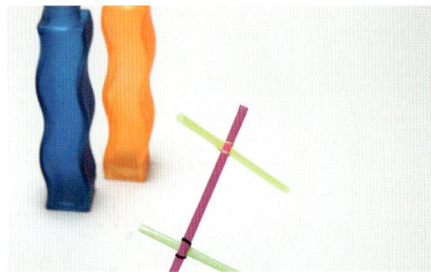

8 Repeat steps 3 to 7 with different sized straws.

9 Continue to add different coloured straws, and place the structure in the vases.

10 Place more straws on different planes to create a three dimensional structure.

11 Cut the stem of the gerberas in water.

12 Place the gerbera in the arrangement.

13 Add a second flower to the arrangement.

14 Place a third flower towards the back for depth.

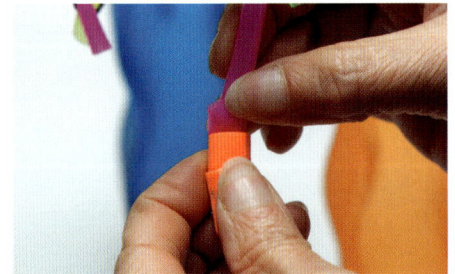

15 Finally, place the coloured erasers on the ends of some of the straws. You may need to bend the straw slightly for a tight fit.

17ⓐ Boys' Day / Children's Day

Kodomo no hi is one of the five seasonal festivals (五節句, gosekku) held on auspicious dates throughout the year (January 1st, March 3rd, May 5th, July 7th, September 9th). Children's Day (Kodomo no hi), previously known as Boy's Day (Tango-no-Sekku), is celebrated in Japan on the 5th of May. The day originated as a celebration to ward off evil spirits for samurai boys.

Traditionally, a Kabuto, Japanese military helmet, is placed on display and Koi Nobori carp streamers are flown, representing a carp's strength against adversity as it swims upstream.

Historically, this day was also known as Ayame no hi (Iris festival). There is a long history of interconnection between Tango-no-Sekku and Ayame no hi. For the Samurai, Iris was considered an auspicious plant due to the shape of its leaves resembling the blade of a katana (sword).

In the past, Irises were also believed to have medicinal properties and to ward off evil. Many people would add Irises to their bath water, drink sake soaked with Iris root, place slices of Iris in their pillows, or weave Iris leaves into the thatched roofs of their homes. In 1948, the Japanese Government renamed the holiday calling it Kodomo no hi (Children's Day) to celebrate the happiness of all children. Although the holiday now includes both boys and girls, the relevance and tradition of Iris and the use of kabuto and armour remains.

MATERIAL

Dutch iris, orchid leaves, small pebbles, kenzan, origami paper

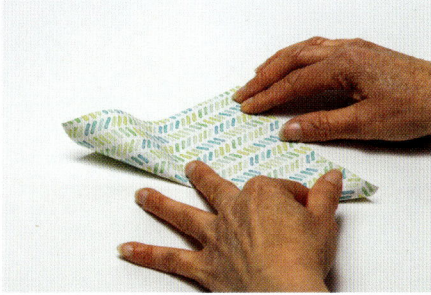

1 Fold the paper in half to form a triangle.

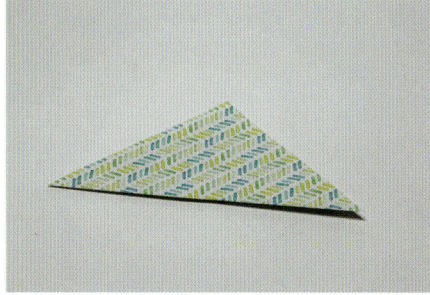

2 Fold origami with care and precision.

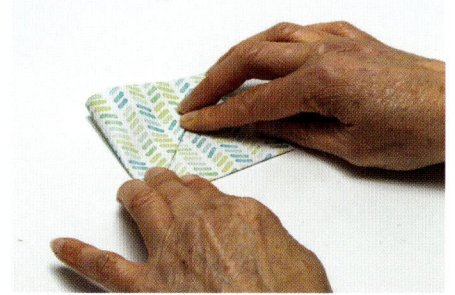

3 Fold each corner to meet the tip of the triangle.

4 Turn the square so that the openings are at the bottom.

5 Fold one side up to meet the top.

6 Repeat step 5 on the other side.

7 Both sides should be equal.

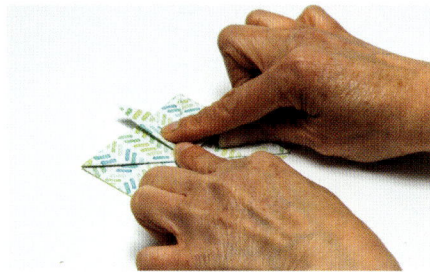

8 Take the tip of one and fold it down. The tip should extend past the edge. Repeat on the other side.

9 Fold the bottom tip towards the top. With the tip of the triangle just below the top of the helmet.

10 Fold the bottom up so that the base is in alignment with the bottom of the helmet.

11 The bottom of the fold should be in alignment with the bottom of the helmet.

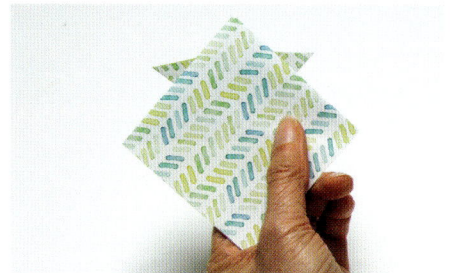

12 Turn the helmet over.

13 Fold the bottom tip up, there should be space between the tip and the top of the helmet.

14 Fold the bottom so that the base is in alignment with the bottom of the helmet.

15 Open slightly.

1 Choose a low flat vase or bowl.

2 Place a kenzan in the vase.

3 Add water to the vase.

4 Rearrange the leaves in groups of 2 and 3.

5 Cut the stem of the iris in water.

6 Place a group of 3 leaves on the kenzan.

7 Add an iris flower.

8 Place a group of 2 leaves in front of the iris flower.

9 The iris should be 'sandwiched' between the 2 groups of leaves.

10 There should be depth and movement to the iris and the leaves.

11 Repeat steps 5 to 10.

12 Add a few stones to cover the kenzan.

13 Finally, add the origami Kabuto.

17 ⓑ Japanese festivals: Girls' Day

In Japan, Hina-matsuri (雛祭り), Girls' Day/ Dolls' Day is celebrated on March 3rd. In homes across the country, elaborate Hina-Ningyou dolls are displayed on red-covered tiered platforms. Although the Hina-Ningyo display in our home is modest, each year my daughters take great pleasure in setting up our Emperor and Empress to celebrate the day.

Alongside our small display of Hina-Ningyo my daughters often place a small ikebana arrangement. Traditionally, peach blossoms are associated with Girls' Day, their bright pink blossoms are a dual reminder of early spring, and young girls.

MATERIAL

*Crataegus monogyna, rapeseed blossoms, lacquered tray,
Hina-Ningyo (Girls' Day dolls)*

1 Place two small vases on a tray.

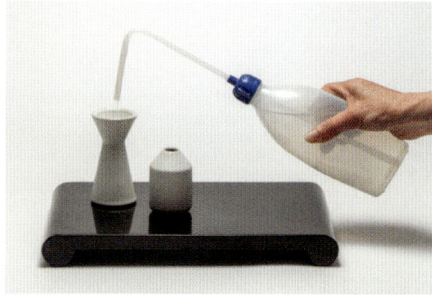

2 Add water to the vases.

3 Cut the flower stems in water.

4 Place a long stem of Rapeseed blossom in one of the vases.

5 Add a small stem of crataegus monogyna close to the rim of the vase.

6 Add a shorter stem of crataegus monogyna to the second vase.

7 Add another short stem of crataegus monogyna for depth.

8 Place a small stem of rapeseed blossom in the second vase. Make sure that it is placed close to the rim.

9 Finally, add the Hina- Ningyo.

17c Tanabata: The Star Festival

One of my daughters' favourite Japanese Festivals is Tanabata (七夕), the Star Festival. Held on the 7th of July, Tanabata, is one of the five seasonal festivals (五節句, gosekku). It celebrates the reunion of star-crossed lovers Orihime and Hikoboshi (in some versions of the story he is also referred to as Kengyū) who are permitted to cross the 'heavenly river' (the Milky Way) and meet just once a year. However, if it rains on the evening of the 7th of July, the lovers, represented by the stars Altair and Vega, cannot meet and must wait another year to be reunited. Rain on the 7th of July is called "The tears of Orihime and Hikoboshi".

Although Sendai hosts the most famous Tanabata festival, we have enjoyed celebrating Tanabata in Hiratsuka along with friends who live close by. There are many brightly coloured decorations associated with Tanabata. Fukingashi, or windsocks, representing an upside-down windswept bonsai tree, Tanzaku, wishes written on strips of coloured paper and hung on branches of bamboo, and Toami, fishing nets, created from paper are some of the decorations on display throughout the town.

MATERIAL

Bamboo, bluebells, origami paper, scissors

1 Fold the paper into a triangle.

2 Fold it once again into a small triangle.

3 Take care not to cut along the open edge.

4 Make slits along one of the folded edges.

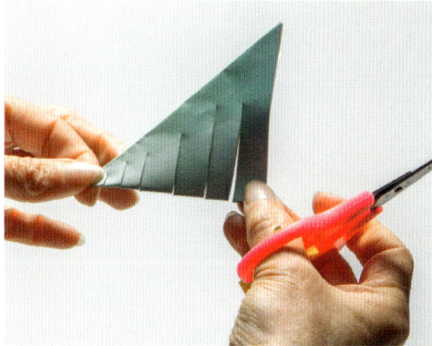

5 Take care not to cut all the way through.

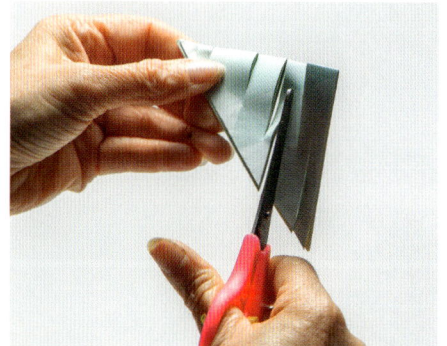

6 Turn the paper over and make slits between the cuts.

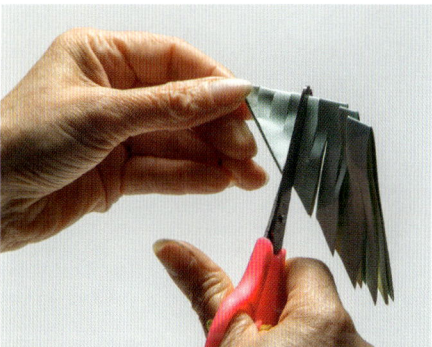

7 Continue cutting to the end.

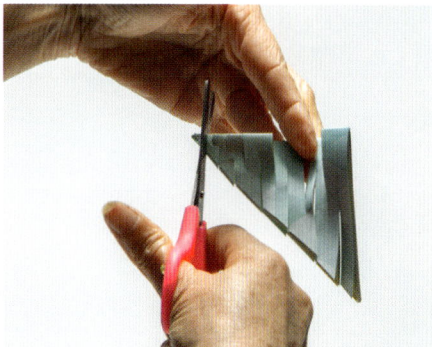

8 Make sure not to cut all the way through the triangle.

9 Carefully open the paper.

10 Take care not to rip the cuts.

11 Open the paper completely.

12 Gently tug on the paper to reveal the fishing net.

1 Choose an appropriate vase. For this arrangement I have chosen a metal watering can.

2 A cross bar is used to hold the materials. Measure the length of the vase.

3 Cut the end of the bamboo to size.

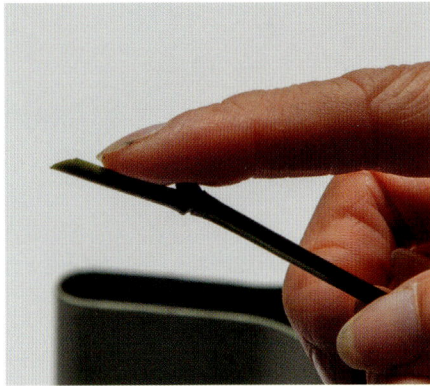

4 One end of the cross bar should be straight and the other cut on an oblique.

5 Insert the crossbar in the vase. This might require a small amount of pressure.

6 Cut the stem of the bamboo in water.

7 To help maintain the leaves, dip the cut end in vinegar for 10 mins.

8 Place the bamboo. It should rest on the cross bar with one end touching the side of the vase.

9 Place a paper fishing net through the leaves.

10 Add a second branch of bamboo.

11 Add water to the vase.

12 Place a second paper net on the second branch. The paper nets should not touch the water.

13 Cut the stems of the blue bells in water.

14 Add the bluebell to the arrangement, close to the main bamboo branch.

15 Add a second flower, towards the front, making sure that the rim of the vase is covered.

18 a Christmas: Massed Christmas baubles

Like many children around the world, my daughters eagerly look forward to Christmas. Although local traditions and customs are different in many of the places that we have lived and visited, there are also things that are similar. When we first arrived in Spain, my eldest daughter was surprised to discover that most of her friends didn't receive gifts on the 25th of December. Instead, they waited patiently until Los Reyes Magos, on January 6th, when the Three Kings would bring their presents. Now in Belgium, both of my daughters are eager for their first Christmas with Saint Nicolas, and the celebrations that will start almost a month prior to those in Spain.

MATERIAL

Weigela, conifer/pine, Christmas baubles, double sided tape/ glue dots

1 Select a vase in a festive colour.

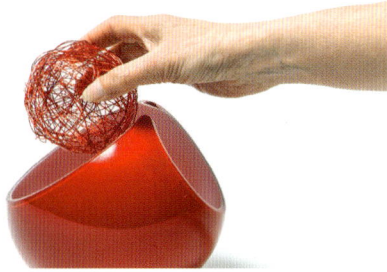

2 Place the wire baubles in the vase.

3 The arrangement will have harmonious imbalance if the baubles are not placed equally.

4 Remove the ends from the baubles.

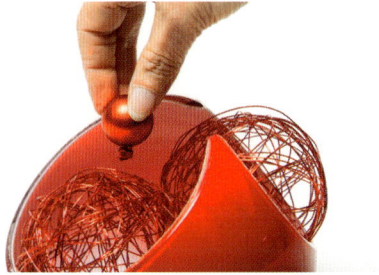

5 Insert the baubles in the wire.

6 Add baubles in a contrasting colour.

7 It may be necessary to affix some baubles using double sided tape.

8 Stick a small piece of tape on the bauble. Remove the backing.

9 Stick the bauble in place.

10 Continue to add baubles to the arrangement.

11 Add water to the vase.

12 Place small branches of conifer/pine between the baubles.

13 Cut the stem of the flower in water.

14 Add a second flower, towards the front, making sure that the rim of the vase is covered.

15 Finally, give the conifer/pine a trim.

18 ⓑ Making a vase with long baubles

Since moving to Belgium my daughters are excited at the prospect of St Nicolas visiting around Christmas time. Unlike Spain where children receive their Christmas presents in January, in Belgium, St. Nicolas (Sint-Niklaas) visits in early December.
On the evening of the 5th of December, children put out their shoes along with a carrot (for St Nicolas' horse). During the night, St. Nicolas rides across the rooftops on horseback and, if the children have been good, the saint will bring them toys and gifts of sweets and mandarins or oranges.

MATERIAL

Ranunculus, conifer/pine, aucuba japonica berries, long Christmas baubles, hot glue gun

1 Remove the tops of the baubles.

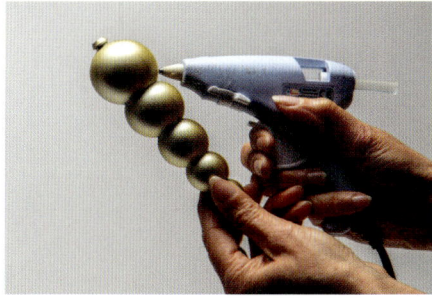

2 Using a hot glue gun, stick the baubles together. Make sure the holes are facing upwards.

3 The baubles should be stable when placed on the table.

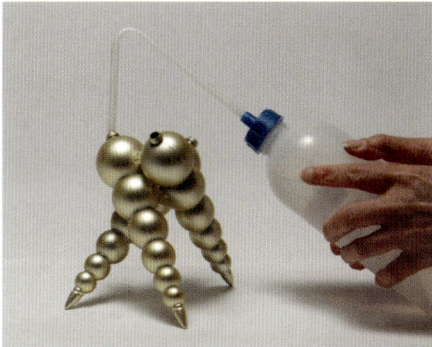

4 Fill the baubles with water.

5 Place a piece of conifer/pine in one of the vase openings.

6 Place a small piece of conifer/pine in another opening.

7 Cut the stem of the flower in water.

8 Add the flower to the arrangement.

9 Place a small stem of aucuba japonica berries at the back of the arrangement to create depth.

Bibliography

Armstrong, K. (2022) Sacred Nature, The Bodley Head, London.

Carrington, D. (2016) Three-quarters of UK children spend less time outdoors than prison inmates – survey. The Guardian, UK. https://www.theguardian.com/environment/2016/mar/25/three-quarters-of-uk-children-spend-less-time-outdoors-than-prison-inmates-survey

Children and Nature report
https://www.wildlifetrusts.org/news/new-report-nature-nurtures-children

Fairclough, M. (2022) Rewilding Childhood, Hay House, London.

Herrigel, G. L. (1987) Zen in the Art of Flower Arrangement, Arkana, UK.

Homma,I., Oizumi, R., and Masaoka, Y. (2015) Effects of Practicing Ikebana on Anxiety and Respiration, Journal of Depression and Anxiety, 4 (3) DOI: 10.4172/2167-1044.1000187 https://www.longdom.org/open-access/effects-of-practicing-ikebana-on-anxiety-and-respiration-29419.html

Inoue, O. (2021) Nature, Man and Flowers: Kado as Philosophical Ikebana, Saihatesha, Japan.

Inoue, O.. (2014) Nature and Art in Ikebana, International Journal of Ikebana Studies (IJIS), December (2).
https://www.academia.edu/30066787/Nature_and_Art_in_Ikebana

Japan - Ministry of Education, Culture Sports, Science and Technology
The Promulgation of the Girls' High School Order https://www.mext.go.jp/b_menu/hakusho/html/others/detail/1317331.htm

Jones, L. (2020) Losing Eden, Allen Lane, London.

Jones, L. and Greenway, K. (2021) The Nature Seed: How to Raise Adventurous and Nurturing Kids, Souvenir Press, U.K.

Joyce, J. (2010). Ulysses, Wordsworth Editions, UK.

Kim, M., Sowndhararajan K et al (2017) Gender Differences in Electroencephalographic Activity in Response to the Earthy Odorants Geosmin and 2-Methylisoborneol, Applied Sciences, 7(9), 876.
https://www.mdpi.com/2076-3417/7/9/876/htm

Kimmerer, R. W. (2017). The Covenant of Reciprocity in The Wiley Blackwell Companion to Religion and Ecology (pp. 368–381). John Wiley & Sons, Ltd.
https://doi.org/10.1002/9781118465523.ch26

Lang, A (2021) Rewilding the Mind: The enactive approach and the Human–nature relationship
https://www.researchgate.net/publication/356166343

Lau, A. (2010), Harnessing the creative potential of Ikebana in promoting personal well-being, Mental Health and Social Inclusion, 14 (3), 30-35.
https://doi.org/10.5042/mhsi.2010.0442

March-Penny, J. (1976) The Master's Book of Ikebana, Samson Low, UK.

Mehl, M. (2001) Women educators and the confucian tradition in Meiji Japan (1868–1912): Miwada Masako and Atomi Kakei , Women's History Review, 10 (4), 579-602, DOI: 10.1080/09612020100200302 To link to this article: https://doi.org/10.1080/09612020100200302

Pickhardt, C. (2014) Teaching resistant adolescents is different from teaching more willing children, Psychology Today. https://www.psychologytoday.com/us/blog/surviving-your-childs-adolescence/201410/teaching-adolescents

Pickhart, C. (2013) Surviving Your Child's Adolescence, Jossey-Bass, U.S.A.

Sasaki, M., Oizumi, R., Homma, A., Masaoka, Y., Iijima, M. et al. (2011) Effects of viewing Ikebana on breathing in humans, Showa Univ Journal of Medical Science. 23, 59-65.

Sheldrake, R., Amos, R., and Reiss, M. J.(2019) Nature Nurtures Children: a summary of research for the wildlife trusts. UCL Institute of Education, London.
https://www.wildlifetrusts.org/sites/default/files/2019-11/Nature%20nurtures%20children%20Summary%20Report%20FINAL.pdf

Shimbo, S. (2018) Nature in Ikebana: Beyond sustainability (いけ花における自然：存続可能性を超えて). International Journal of Ikebana Studies (IJIS), 6, 55- 60.

Sogetsu Foundation (April 2009) Sogetsu Teachers Association Members Guide, Sogetsu Bunkajigyo Co., Ltd.

Sparnon, N. (1984) Creative Japanese Flower Arrange-ment, Shufunotomo Co. Ltd, Tokyo

Stamm, J. (2022) The Way of Flowers.
https://www.lionsroar.com/the-way-of-flowers/

Stuart-Smith, S. (2020) The Well Gardened Mind - Rediscovering Nature in the Modern World, William Collins, London.

Teshigahara, A. (2009) Teaching Ikebana to Children: led by Iemoto Akane Teshigahara, So Newsletter- For Overseas Members of Sogetsu Teachers Association August/September, 197

Teshigahara, K. (1965) Space and Colour in Japanese Flower Arrangements, Kodansha Intl. Ltd. Japan.

U.S. Department of Agriculture
https://www.myplate.gov/

Yokoi, T. (1986) Ikebana - Fruits and Vegetables, Shufunotomo Co., Ltd. Tokyo, Japan.

Author Louise Worner, www.louiseworner.com

Photography Ben Huybrechts, www.ikebana.be

Final editing Katrien Van Moerbeke

Lay-out Group Van Damme, www.groupvandamme.eu

Published by Stichting Kunstboek bv, Legeweg 165, BE-8020 Oostkamp,
Tel. +32 50 46 19 10
info@stichtingkunstboek.com, www.stichtingkunstboek.com

Printed in the EU

ISBN 978-90-5856-716-1

D/2023/6407/13

NUR 421

© Louise Worner 2023

© Ben Huybrechts 2023

© Stichting Kunstboek 2023